9/06

Hispanic Heritage

Hispanic Heritage

Title List

Mason Crest Publishers Inc.

370 Reed Road

Broomall, Pennsylvania 19008

(866) MCP-BOOK (toll free)

First printing

1 2 3 4 5 6 7 8 9 10

Library of Congress Cataloging-in-Publication Data

Makosz, Rory.

 Latino arts and their influence on the United States : songs, dreams, and dances / by Rory Makosz.

    p. cm. —— (Hispanic heritage)

 Includes index.

 ISBN 1-59084-938-8   ISBN 1-59084-924-8 (series)

 1. Arts, Latin American—Juvenile literature. 2. Arts, American—Latin American influences—Juvenile literature. I. Title. II. Hispanic heritage (Philadelphia, Pa.)

 NX501.5.M35 2005

 700'.89'68073——dc22

                           2004022968

Produced by Harding House Publishing Service, Inc., Vestal, NY.

Interior design by Dianne Hodack and MK Bassett-Harvey.

Cover design by Dianne Hodack.

Chapter 5 adapted from Kenneth McIntoshês contributions.

Printed and bound in the Hashemite Kingdom of Jordan.

Latino Arts
and Their Influence
on the United States

Songs, Dreams, and Dances

by Rory Makosz

Mason Crest Publishers

Philadelphia

Contents

Introduction

by José E. Limón, Ph.D.

ven before there was a United States, Hispanics were present in what would become this country. Beginning in the sixteenth century, Spanish explorers traversed North America, and their explorations encouraged settlement as early as the sixteenth century in what is now northern New Mexico and Florida, and as late as the mid-eighteenth century in what is now southern Texas and California.

Later, in the nineteenth century, following Spain's gradual withdrawal from the New World, Mexico in particular established its own distinctive presence in what is now the southwestern part of the United States, a presence reinforced in the first half of the twentieth century by substantial immigration from that country. At the close of the nineteenth century, the U.S. war with Spain brought Cuba and Puerto Rico into an interactive relationship with the United States, the latter in a special political and economic affiliation with the United States even as American power influenced the course of almost every other Latin American country.

The books in this series remind us of these historical origins, even as each explores the present reality of different Hispanic groups. Some of these books explore the contemporary social origins—what social scientists call the "push" factors—behind the accelerating Hispanic immigration to America: political instability, economic underdevelopment and crisis, environmental degradation, impoverished or wholly absent educational systems, and other circumstances contribute to many Latin Americans deciding they will be better off in the United States.

And, for the most part, they will be. The vast majority come to work and work very hard, in order to earn better wages than they would back home. They fill significant labor needs in the U.S. economy and contribute to the economy through lower consumer prices and sales taxes.

When they leave their home countries, many immigrants may initially fear that they are leaving behind vital and important aspects of their home cultures: the Spanish language, kinship ties, food, music, folklore, and the arts. But as these books also make clear, culture is a fluid thing, and these native cultures are not only brought to America, they are also replenished in the United States in fascinating and novel ways. These books further suggest to us that Hispanic groups enhance American culture as a whole.

Our country—especially the young, future leaders who will read these books—can only benefit by the fair and full knowledge these authors provide about the socio-historical origins and contemporary cultural manifestations of America's Hispanic heritage.

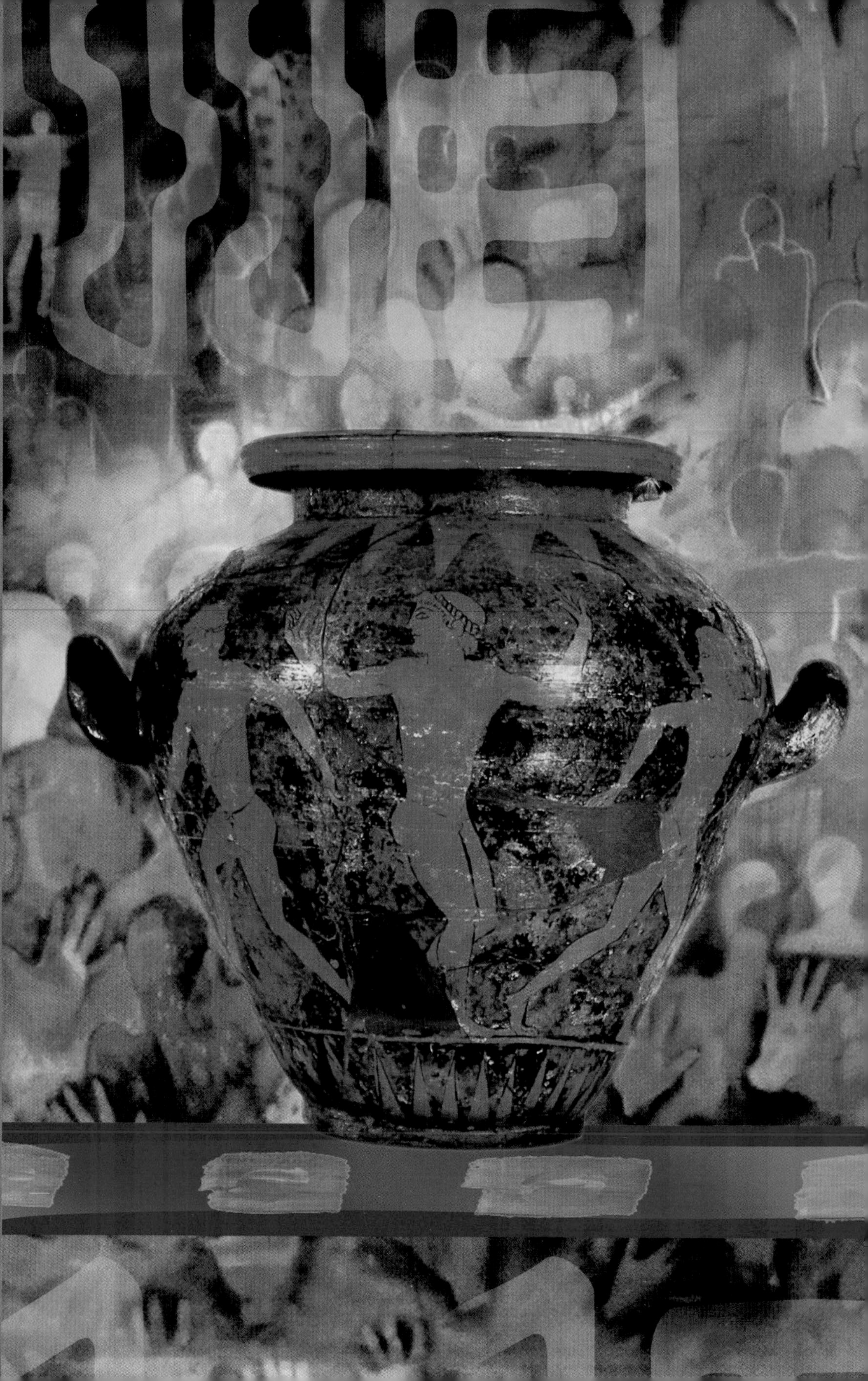

Expressions of Identity: The Bond Between Culture and Art

Throughout time and across the globe, human civilization has used art as a powerful tool of communication. For thousands upon thousands of years, people have been creating things—from poems to pottery, music to grand buildings—that we call art. But certainly not everything that humans make can be called art. So what makes one object, for example, a great work of art, while another is just an object?

Artwork
A mural in El Centro Cultural Tijuana combines Native influences with modern techniques to express the power and creativity of Latino arts. This mural is used as the recurring motif for the chapter openers in this book.

9

An early Egyptian portrayal of Queen Nefertiti

If this is a question you have trouble answering, you are not alone. Some of the world's greatest thinkers have tried to define art, and there remains no single definition on which everyone would agree. We can look at paintings, sculptures, costumes, poems, songs, dances, and many other creations, and conclude that each one of these things, if possessing certain qualities, can be a work of art. So what are the qualities that can elevate a creation from being just an ordinary thing to being art?

One of the most useful definitions of art is also one of the oldest. The Greek philosopher Aristotle described the purpose of art as being "to represent not the outward appearance of things, but their inward significance." What Aristotle meant was that a thing's artistic quality does not just come from what it *looks like*. The artistic quality also comes from what the thing *means*. In Aristotle's view, an ordinary object, even if it was beautiful and pleasing to look at, could not be art unless it communicated some deeper meaning to the person viewing the object. This may be why art is often such a personal thing: something that has meaning to me may not have meaning to you. For example, you may think a painting of your dog is a beautiful work of art, while another person may think the painting is just a pretty picture. Your opinions about the painting may be different based on whether or not you see any *inward significance* in the painting's *outward appearance*. Who knows? Perhaps if the other person knew and understood your dog the way you do, they would think the painting is a work of art too!

Although many people disagree over what precisely "art" is, few would dispute art's importance as a mode of expression and communication. Through an image, a song, a piece of writing, or other art form, people can express an enormous variety of ideas, memories, emotions, and events. When looking at Pablo Picasso's famous painting, *Guernica*, for example, one can begin

The ancient Greeks made ordinary objects into things of beauty.

An artist that lived long ago created this painting of a reindeer on a cave wall.

to imagine what it may have felt like to have one's life torn apart by the Spanish Civil War. When watching a performance of Shakespeare's *Romeo and Juliet*, one can understand what it would feel like to experience great love and great loss. The inward significance of a piece of art may be personal or it may have meaning to a large group of people. In this book we will be dealing with art that, although it may also be personal, also tells the story of a larger group of people: Latinos. In particular, we will discuss how Latino artists have used their work to communicate concepts that are important to their own communities and cultures and how Latino art has influenced the United States. Unfortunately, because there are so many Latino artists and because Latino art has such a rich history, it is impossible to talk about every artist or even every form of Latino art. For that reason, we will concentrate on those aspects of Latino culture that have had the greatest impact on the larger society and the individual artists who have played the biggest roles in bringing this culture to the United States. Before we do this, however, there are some important concepts about culture and art that we should explore further.

spectrum: a broad range of different items, often ordered from most similar to least similar.

Identity, Community, and Culture: Important Concepts

here are about 6.5 billion people in the world, and each one is unique. Even if you had enough time to meet every single person, you would never meet another person who is just like you. What you would find is a *spectrum* of people, some of them a lot like you, some of them a little bit like you, and some whom you would think are very different and perhaps even very strange. Chances are you've already met enough people to know just how different they can be. But have you thought much about *why* people can be so different, or, for that matter, so similar?

People are similar or different depending on the number and types of characteristics they share. Our characteristics define who we are and include things like our physical features, our personalities, our likes and dislikes, and our values and beliefs. Taken together, a person's characteristics all add up to form his or her identity. If you think of each characteristic of a person as being a building block, then that person's identity is like a house

13

stereotype: a set of characteristics that are applied to a person or group based on that person or group's classification (e.g., Latino, Caucasian, American, etc.). Stereotypes are not necessarily accurate.

made out of those building blocks. Every person has her own identity, even if she shares many characteristics with and is very similar to someone else.

Individuals aren't the only ones who have identities. Groups of people can have identities as well. A group of people with a shared identity is often called a community, and the characteristics the group shares are called their culture. Culture is a word used to describe group characteristics like values, traditions, history, and beliefs. Just as an individual identity is like a house made out of many building blocks, a culture is like a neighborhood made out of many houses. Similarly, just as every individual has her own unique identity, every community has its own distinct culture. It is important to remember that when we talk about individuals and communities, we are talking about people, and when we talk about identities and cultures, we are talking about characteristics.

One of the powerful things about culture is that it can tell us some of the characteristics that a group's individual members are likely to have, and the more we know about that culture, the more accurate our predictions about its members are likely to be. For example, if we know that Juan is a member of a competitive surfing team, we can guess that he is probably a pretty good surfer, that he can probably swim well, and that he probably lives near a beach somewhere. If we also know that surfing culture is typically relaxed and fun-loving, we may expect Juan to be relaxed and fun-loving too. On the other hand, we have to be careful not to guess too much about individuals based on their group identity or culture. After all, each person is still an individual even if he is a member of a larger group. Just because we know Juan is a surfer doesn't allow us to guess what kind of food he prefers, what kind of music he listens to, or what he looks like.

"Primitive" Cuban art reveals the pride and vitality of Cuban culture.

When we make assumptions about a person or try to guess what that person is like based on what group that person belongs to, we may be using a *stereotype*. A stereotype is like an image or set of characteristics that we associate with a particular group of people or things. It does not matter if the group actually *has* these characteristics, only that we *believe* it does. To stereotype someone means to assume that, because that person belongs to a particular group, she must have certain characteristics.

It is often a natural reaction to use stereotypes because they can help us to understand and process information in the world very quickly. However, stereotypes can also be extremely dangerous. If you have a negative stereotype of a certain group, you may avoid its

15

members and miss out on meeting great people, learning important things, and making new friends. You may even treat the members of the group differently without realizing it and make judgments about them that are incorrect and unfair. This is why it is important to remember that culture, while it can have a very strong influence in shaping a person's individual identity, does not shape all of that person's characteristics. The communities you belong to have an impact on what you are like as a person and how you perceive the world around you, but they are not the only things that determine who you are. Individuals take some aspects of their communities' cultures and incorporate those characteristics into their own identities as they grow and learn, but you cannot guess all of a person's individual characteristics just by knowing what communities and cultures that individual is a member of.

Speaking Through Art: Communicating Culture

An artist reveals as much about himself as his subject.

As an individual, you have many ways of presenting your unique identity to the world. You may express yourself through the way you dress, the way you speak, the type of music you listen to, the sports or games you like to play, your favorite color, and numerous other actions, thoughts, likes, or dislikes. All these things help the people around you identify who you are. Other people, your friends for example, know who you are based on their own experiences of what you are like and the things you like to do.

Communities Within Communities

ommunities come in different shapes and sizes, and one person could be a member of numerous communities and cultures. You and the students in your class, for example, are a small community, and you all share some characteristics that make up your classroom culture. But your classroom overlaps with other communities. You and your classmates may be in different clubs, different sports teams, and different families. In other words, although you all belong to your classroom community, you may also belong to additional communities that are different from each other.

Smaller communities can also fit inside larger ones. Your classroom community fits into your school, which fits into your city, which fits into your state, and so on. As the community gets bigger and a larger number of more *diverse* people are included, it becomes harder to identify the characteristics that make up the community's culture. For example, you can probably think of several things that you and the other members of your family have in common. If you look at the United States as a community, however, how many characteristics can you think of that would accurately describe every single person in that community?

rt not only allows one individual to communicate with another or one community to understand another, but it also allows an individual or community to communicate across time. Through art, ideas can be passed from one generation to the next, even after the original artist is long gone. History may be told through literature or music. Important events, beliefs, or values may be represented in paintings or poems. Traditions may be passed down through dances or songs. Communities embrace works of art that they feel express their values or cultures, and these works become a part of that culture. Even if the characteristics of the group change and evolve over time, by using art to pass traditions from old to young, the strongest elements of a culture can be preserved. Even if a community disappears or dies off, the art it leaves behind may allow its important stories to continue to be told.

Communities express themselves in many of the same basic ways individuals do. People from the same community may dress in a similar way, like a certain kind of music, follow a certain sport, or cook a certain type of food. Of course, not every individual in the community necessarily expresses themselves in the same way (remember about stereotypes!), but generally the things that define one community from another are the same things that help define you to your friends.

integrated: two or more things united into a whole.

One of the ways in which both individuals and communities express some of their most important thoughts, feelings, interests, and histories is through art. Art can take many forms. Perhaps you have already tried your hand at painting, writing, playing a musical instrument, or another form of art. If you have, what did you paint? What did you write about? What instrument did you play, and what kind of music did you make? Your answers to these questions reflect choices you have made—choices that express your own identity. The choices you made may also reflect aspects of your culture. Sometimes an entire community will appreciate a certain work of art produced by one of its members. Usually this admiration exists because the work has some special meaning for that community or represents some aspect of its culture. When this happens, that work of art can become a symbol of the community and a way for the community to communicate its culture to others.

Poster art can reveal a culture's values and pride.

There are as many different styles of art as there are cultures in the world. Sometimes, however, it can be difficult to tell where one culture ends and another one begins. This is especially true when two communities come from similar backgrounds or have a great deal of interaction with each other. Where two communities are closely associated with each other, or are *integrated*, it is inevitable that some of the characteristics of each community will rub off on the other and their cultures

protectorate: a state that is partly controlled by or under the influence of another.

simultaneous: done at the same time.

will change. These changes are often reflected in the art the communities produce. Sometimes the two communities not only interact with each other, but they actually merge, creating one new culture with some of the characteristics of each old one and some brand new characteristics of its own. One of the places where there has been a great deal of cultural integration and where many artistic styles have come together to create something totally new is Latin America.

Latinos and the Latin Explosion

Latin America includes Mexico, all of the countries of Central and South America, and the islands of the Caribbean. In most of these countries, the cultures that exist today are not just the products of one or two communities coming together, but are more likely to be the result of three or four or even five different cultures all influencing each other or merging into one. As a result, the art that Latin American culture has produced is unique in that it blends the styles of many diverse cultures. In the course of this book, we will look at how this blending of cultures came about, and we will also examine how the arts that these cultures have produced have influenced the larger community and culture of the United States.

People of Latin American descent living in the United States are collectively referred to as Latinos. With over 35 million individuals, Latinos are the largest minority group in the country.

Mexican folkart is popular across America.

In fact, if you include Puerto Rico, which is an American *protectorate*, the number is about 40 million. That's more people than live in the entire state of California and more than twice as many as live in the state of New York. Not surprisingly, Latino art and culture have had a big influence in the United States.

Over the last decade, Latino culture has become far more prominent in the United States. Many American observers call this cultural trend the "Latin Explosion." What they are talking about is the sudden and *simultaneous* emergence of a number of influential Latino artists in American popular culture. Over a relatively short span of time, Latinos like Ricky Martin and Jennifer Lopez began dominating American popular music. Latino actors like Benicio Del Toro and Salma Hayek started playing lead roles in major American movies. Several of these movies were even based on the lives of famous Latin Americans, particularly women such as Eva Peron, Selena Quintanilla, and Frida Kahlo. The reasons behind this recent trend are not really clear. It could be that the growing Latino population is simply producing more artists or is creating a larger demand for products with familiar names and faces. Or it could be that the wider American commu-

The black pottery of Mexico has gained world recognition.

nity has found something in Latino art that really appeals to people from a broad range of backgrounds.

Whatever the reason for the increase in Latino influence, the term "explosion" is somewhat misleading, giving the impression that Latino art has had little impact in the United States until very recently. This is simply not the case, and there have been several "explosions" of Latino culture in the United States over the past hundred years. In fact, Latino culture has been around and has been influential since before the United States even came into being. However, before we have a look at the influence that Latino art has had in shaping American culture over the years, we should understand the diverse roots of Latino culture itself.

Habla Español

arta (ahr-tah): art

cultura (cool-too-rah): culture

gente (hane-tay): people

22

Understanding the Term "Latino"

Many people use the term "Latino" to refer to any person of Latin American descent who lives in the United States. Technically, however, this is not an accurate use of the term. Latino is actually a linguistic term; it concerns language. Only people who are descended from a Latin American culture that speaks a Latin-based language (like Spanish, Portuguese, or French) are considered Latino. The Native peoples of Latin America are not considered Latino even though theirs were the first Latin American communities. Similarly, people from English-speaking countries in Latin America, like Jamaica, are not considered Latino.

Sometimes you may hear the terms "Latino" and "Hispanic" used interchangeably, but they are not quite the same. "Hispanic" refers to people who speak Spanish or have a Spanish background. While Spanish is the dominant language in most Latin American countries, it is not the only language spoken in this vast region. In Brazil, for example, which is the largest Latin American country, most people speak Portuguese. Portuguese-speaking Brazilians are not considered Hispanic, but they are considered Latino. Furthermore, the terms Hispanic and Latino were coined and are typically used only in the United States.

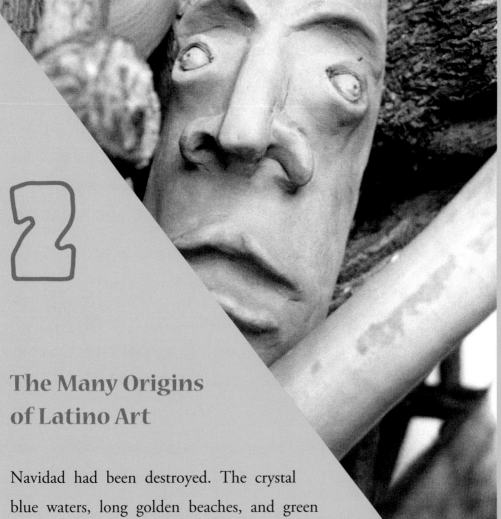

2

The Many Origins of Latino Art

Navidad had been destroyed. The crystal blue waters, long golden beaches, and green treed mountains remained just as Christopher Columbus and his crew had left them when they set sail from *Española* less than a year before. But the small group of simple buildings fortified by wooden walls, a settlement they had built just before their departure and which was the first European community in the *New World*, was no more. All that remained was a scattering of stones, sticks, and scraps. Thirty-nine men had lived there, left behind while their comrades sailed home to Spain. They were all strong sailors, and all of them had been in good health. Now, if they were to be found in Navidad at all, they were to be found only as ghosts.

New World: the territories of the Americas "discovered" by Columbus and other explorers.

25

n 1492 Columbus and his company of Spanish explorers had discovered an island paradise in the Caribbean Sea. Columbus had named the island Española because it reminded him of Spain (España). For almost a month, he and his men had stayed there, replenishing their energy after a long and difficult voyage. The island had an abundance of food ripe for the picking, and its natives were peaceful, friendly, and helpful. The Taino, as these people were called, were short, dark haired, dark skinned, and lived in simple huts made out of palm fronds and straw. They received the Spanish warmly and were eager to trade with them as the Spanish had many goods the Taino had never seen. The Taino had gold; something for which the sailors had an *insatiable* appetite.

In their language, Taino meant "good" or "noble," words that described them well. When it came time for Columbus and his men to leave Española, the *Santa Maria*, one of their large sailing ships, ran afoul of a reef and was wrecked beyond repair. Had it not been for the help of the noble Taino, who waded into the water alongside the distressed Spaniards, much of the ship's valuable cargo might have been lost. Without the *Santa Maria*, there was no way that all of Columbus's men could make the return voyage to Spain, so thirty-nine were left behind. They built a small settlement and named it Navidad. The natives and the Spaniards worked together to salvage the wood from the wrecked ship, and it was this wood that was used in the making of the fort. Confident that his men were well taken care of, Columbus set course for Spain knowing he would soon return. He had not expected to return to a scene of destruction and thirty-nine dead men.

The patterns and colors of Spain came with the Spanish explorers to the Americas.

Street musicians in Los Angeles call to mind an ancient heritage.

aonabo, a Taino chief, had never seen anything like the Spanish ships that arrived on the shores of his island, an island his people called *Ayiti*, which meant "land of mountains." He had never seen people like the Spanish before either: light-skinned and bearded with strange clothes and customs. He had never heard the words they spoke and did not understand them. Still, while they had been strange, they had not been dangerous like the Caribs, who threatened war and sometimes appeared on the island. Some of the Taino hoped that, with their metal weapons, the newcomers might help them against these invasions. For now though, the Taino were content to trade with the Spanish.

Spanish goods were unusual, highly valued, and freely given in exchange for the gold the Taino had taken from the streams and fashioned into jewelry. The sailors seemed strangely obsessed with the yellow metal. After a while the sailors left, leaving behind a small group for whom there was no room on their boats. It was not long after this that things changed.

As time went by, the Spanish men who had stayed became aggressive both with each other and with their island hosts. They argued and fought among themselves. They pursued the Taino women, sometimes using force to subdue them. They were quick to employ their superior weapons, guns, and swords to make the Taino do what they wanted. The hosts were quickly becoming servants. For weeks things worsened until finally Caonabo had seen enough and decided to take action. He led an attack against Navidad, and when it was all over the Spanish lay dead and their settlement destroyed. With their hostility and the threat of their weapons gone, peace returned to Ayiti. It did not last long.

Columbus returned within the year and discovered what had happened at Navidad. This time, he had brought more ships, seventeen of them, and more than a thousand men. The Spanish also brought horses, dogs, farm animals, and more weapons and armor made of iron. Columbus and his crew were not explorers on this voyage but conquerors. They had come for gold. They had come for slaves. They had come to stay.

The Spanish arsenal was overpowering, and it was not long before Caonabo was captured and the Natives of Española were enslaved. The Taino were forced into hard labor panning for gold or working in fields. Many were worked to their graves, and many others who survived the grueling conditions succumbed to European diseases like smallpox. They tried

Catholicism: the philosophy of the Catholic Church and Catholic religion.

conversion: changing one thing into another. For example, religious conversion involves changing a person's beliefs from one religion to another.

to fight back, but there was nothing they could do. They were dying by the hundreds.

Within ten years, so many of the natives had died under their brutal masters that the Spanish had to bring in slaves from Africa to replace them. Soon there were more Africans on the island than Taino, and the Taino were continuing to die off in large numbers. Desperate to escape the abuse, some chose to take their own lives rather than suffer under the Spanish. It took less than a century for the island's Natives, who had once numbered in the hundreds of thousands, to disappear from the earth forever. Spain now had a foothold in the new world and driven by a lust for riches was about to stride across the rest of the Americas in waves of conquest and bloodshed.

Storming the Continent

pain had set its hungry eyes on the New World, and Española was the base from which it would launch and fuel its invasion of the Americas. Spanish explorers like Juan Ponce de León and Juan de Esquivel led successful conquests of Puerto Rico, Cuba, Jamaica, and Florida. Other explorers, like Hernando de Soto, traveled into the mainland of Central and South America. Along the way countless Native peoples were killed and their wealth and lands stolen. The survivors were converted to *Catholicism* and forced to become Spanish servants.

Even the mightiest of America's early civilizations could not stop the Spanish conquests. The great Aztec Empire, which dominated the land of present-day Mexico, had long ruled over other tribes in the area and sacrificed them to the Aztec gods.

Remnants of a Spanish Heritage

lmost all of the countries of Latin America that were conquered by Spain still retain Spanish as their official language and Catholicism as the dominant religion. Although the Spanish were ultimately defeated in North America, and although English is the only official language of the United States, many American states, including Florida, California, Colorado, and Nevada still bear the names given to them by the Spanish. In fact, the name America comes from that of an Italian explorer, Amerigo Vespucci, who sailed with the Spanish fleets to the New World.

Hernán Cortéz led an army comprised of Spaniards and of Natives who were tired of living under the Aztecs into the capital city of Tenochtitlán and defeated the Aztecs and their emperor Montezuma. Fifteen years later, Peru's mighty Incan Empire had also fallen, a result of the trickery of Spanish explorer Francisco Pizarro. Within the next decade, the third of the great American civilizations, the Maya, were also conquered by Spain.

The Spanish trail of destruction, religious *conversion*, settlement, and theft continued

*waned: declined slowly
or faded away.*

to blaze across the Americas in all directions. During this time, however, a new player entered the game. Spain's neighbor, Portugal, decided it too might have something to gain in the New World. The Portuguese had first come to Brazil in 1500 and had returned from time to time since then, but it took about thirty years for them to realize the true potential of what they had discovered. Brazil did not possess the riches of gold and silver that other parts of the New World did, and there were too few people living there for the Portuguese to capture and use or sell as slaves. But what Brazil did possess was rich soil, perfect for growing sugarcane. Soon, on the backs of African slaves brought in on great Portuguese ships, Brazil became the largest sugar producer in the world, and Portuguese settlements expanded out over the land. A new source of wealth was being exploited, and it would not be long before Europe's other great nations decided they wanted a piece of the action.

Late Arrivals to the New World

or about a hundred years, Spain and Portugal had the New World more or less to themselves, but things were happening in Europe that would change all that as the 1500s came to a close. In 1580, Spain conquered Portugal, and Portugal remained under Spanish control for another sixty years. In that time, Spanish and Portuguese military power *waned*, and other European nations became more powerful. As a result, both Spain and Portugal were less able to defend their newfound territory, and other European powers started moving in. The enor-

The art and culture of the Native world is evident in modern Latino street art.

exploit: take advantage of.

incursions: entries or invasions into a territory or domain.

East Indians: Native people from the East Indies.

anti-Semitism: a philosophy that dislikes or is against the Jewish religion or Jewish people generally.

mous potential riches of the New World were becoming increasingly apparent, and those nations who could *exploit* them were eager to do so. Three nations in particular started to make *incursions* into Portuguese and Spanish territory: the Dutch, French, and British.

In the 1600s the British captured the Caribbean islands of St. Kitts and Jamaica while the French took control of Martinique and Guadeloupe and then settled on the mainland to the north of Brazil in what is now called French Guiana. The Dutch landed just to the west of them in present-day Suriname, and Dutch traders quickly built trading posts and settlements there. The British followed the Dutch and French onto the mainland, setting up next to them in Guyana. All of these groups were interested in the wealth to be had from sugar plantations, and all of them brought slaves from Africa to work their fields. Slavery in these areas was not abolished until the mid-1800s, and when it was, *East Indians* were brought in to work as cheap labor in near slave-like conditions, adding yet another culture to what had by then become a very mixed area.

In the 1700s, British and French attention turned to North America. The Dutch lost interest in exploration of the New World and in the dwindling production of their sugar enterprise. Other groups, however, continued to trickle into Latin America. Argentina, for example, is now home to about half of South America's 500,000 Jewish people, many of whom came to escape rising *anti-Semitism* in Europe. There are also many people of Italian descent scattered throughout Latin America, as well as people from Arab countries like Syria. There are about 1.5 million people of Japanese descent living in South America as well.

Of these late arrivals, many would not fit into the definition of Latino. Even so, with them came diverse cultures with differ-

A Complicated Identity

Because of Puerto Rico's special relationship with the United States, Puerto Ricans are born with American citizenship, and many choose to move to America. As a result, many Puerto Ricans see themselves as having two homes, and there are almost as many Puerto Ricans living in the United States (3.4 million) as there are in Puerto Rico (3.8 million). It was the desire to unite their two identities into one that gave birth to the term Nuyorican (New York-Puerto Rican) in New York. The term Nuyorican has now transcended its initial New York borders, and there are people of Puerto Rican descent throughout the United States who identify with this particular culture and this particular name.

ent languages, styles of cooking, kinds of clothing, forms of music and dance, and stories to tell. They also brought new customs, beliefs, and religions. While the major influences in creating Latino culture have been Spanish, African, Portuguese, and the Native populations, smaller groups also helped shaped this new way of life.

Anglo: an English-speaking Caucasian in the United States who is not of Hispanic origin. In Canada, it refers to an English-speaking person in Canada, especially in Quebec.

Latino Culture Emerges in the United States

By now you have an idea of just how many cultures have influenced the people of Latin America. Over the last five hundred years, these diverse groups have mixed to form cultures unlike those in any other part of the world. In the United States, people descended from these groups form the Latino population, which is made up of many different communities. Some Latinos are recent immigrants. Some have lived in the United States for generations. Today, Latino cultures in the United States continue to evolve. Chicanos and Nuyoricans are just two prominent examples of Latino communities in the United States.

Today, many Mexicans and Mexican Americans living in the United States identify themselves as Chicanos. This term refers to people of Mexican descent who subscribe to a philosophy called *Chicanismo*. Chicanismo emerged in California in the 1960s. Its inspiration came from a set of conferences at Loyola University in Los Angeles in which a number of Mexican student organizations came together to discuss the role of Mexican students in an *Anglo* education system. The Chicano *movimiento* also traces its roots to the National Farm Workers Association and its leader César Chávez, who went on strike to protest the poor pay and working conditions of migrant laborers, many of whom were Mexican or Mexican American. These events brought a newfound sense of pride and unity to California's Mexican population, and soon many Mexican Americans across the country identified themselves as Chicanos.

Latino arts are seen on sidewalks in Los Angeles.

According to Chicanismo philosophy, Mexican Americans are a people struggling to retain their identity in an Anglo country with Anglo institutions. Many Chicano people feel they have been denied opportunities because of their background and language and have been pushed to the edges of society where their culture is unappreciated and nearly invisible. The goal of Chicanismo is to fully embrace Mexican identity and heritage as an integral part of the community's life in America. Chicano people take pride in the history, language, culture, and achievements of the Mexican people. Chicanos aim not only to succeed in America, but to succeed in America as Mexicans who understand and are proud of their heritage.

Another distinct Latino group sprang up on the opposite side of the country in New

Cut paper and other Latino crafts are displayed in a California shop.

York City's Puerto Rican neighborhoods. Just as Mexican Americans struggled with their identity in an English-speaking America in the 1960s, Puerto Ricans were engaged in a struggle to define their culture as well. Because Puerto Rico is an American protectorate and Puerto Ricans are born with American citizenship, many people of Puerto Rican descent have a rather split sense of identity; they feel torn between being Puerto Rican and being American. In New York, many people of Puerto Rican descent brought these two identities together to form a new identity: Nuyorican.

Nuyoricans embrace their identity as a people who live between cultures. They may not speak the same Spanish that native Puerto Ricans speak, and they recognize that their history in the United States has been largely spent struggling for equality and recognition. What they have created with the term "Nuyorican" is a term that acknowledges the multiple parts of their identities as equally important.

Together with other Latin American cultures, new communities like the Chicanos, Nuyoricans, and many others have had a profound influence on the culture of the United States. As Latino communities have arrived or have sought to discover their identities, they have expressed themselves through art. We will now look at the art that these complex histories and people have produced and how it has changed the world in which we live today. We will begin by looking at the areas where Latinos have arguably had the biggest impact: the world of music and dance.

Habla Español

isla (ees-lah): island

historia (ees-tore-ee-ah): history

3

Body and Soul: The Dances and Music of Latin America

Of all the different kinds of art that Latinos have produced, few have had a more visible impact in America than Latino music and dance. In fact, you are probably already familiar with Latino music even if you don't realize it. You may be surprised to discover just how many different kinds of Latino dance and music you have already heard of.

Young Puerto Rican dancers

As we saw in chapter 2, today's Latino cultures arose from a blending of many cultures. Each of these cultures contributed its distinct artistic traditions to Latin America. The Spanish and Portuguese brought new sounds, particularly from string instruments like fiddles and guitars, and new styles of dance that involved tapping shoes against the floor or waving bright scarves in the air to add flourish and color. Africans brought a rich mix of rhythmic music and drumming as well as exciting and energetic dance forms. The Native musicians of Latin America relied heavily on flutes and other wind instruments, and these sounds also found their place in the new forms of music that emerged. As other groups arrived from all over the world, they too brought their unique cultural contributions. Even forms of polka, which has Czech and Polish origins, and waltz, which has Austrian origins, have their place within the spectrum of Latin American music and dance!

From the Sound Waves to the Dance Halls

arly in the 1900s, the American music scene was far from being the creative and influential force in the world it is today. Rock and roll wasn't born yet, and jazz and blues were only in their infancy. Latin American music was a completely foreign concept in most parts of the United States, except in the Southwest where Latino communities lived largely ignored by their Anglo neighbors.

Latin American sounds began creeping into America at the

The Birth of Entertainment Radio

ango may not have achieved its enormous popularity if it wasn't for a fairly new medium in America: entertainment radio. Unlike most radio at the time, which broadcast news and information, entertainment radio concentrated on music, comedy, and stories. One of the most famous pioneers of this new medium was a Latino from New York named Vincent Lopez. He was a bandleader and pianist during the 1920s and 1930s who rose to the top of the New York music scene by playing in prominent hotels and cafes. Through his long-running radio program, Lopez reached a very large audience of people from all walks of life. His show not only furthered the influence of Latino music in America but also made radio more popular throughout the country.

very beginning of the twentieth century, but the first major wave of Latin American music didn't hit the United States until the 1920s and 1930s. It was during this time that Argentina's spicy *tango* became a major hit across the world. At first, people both in Argentina and abroad viewed the flirtatious and seductive dance and its accompanying dramatic music as highly immoral. In fact, it was only after the tango became a worldwide sensation that it was widely accepted in Argentina, the country of its birth. As the tango's popularity spread, young couples eager to learn and strut their stuff packed into dancehalls around the world. Today there are even French and Finnish versions of the tango, and the dance is featured in genres like figure skating and synchronized swimming.

One of those responsible for starting the tango "invasion" was Xavier Cugat, a Spanish-born musician who had been raised in Cuba and who moved to New York City—a hub for both Latino immigrants and musicians. Cugat not only helped make the tango a sensation, he also introduced America to other Latin dances like the *rumba*—a Cuban musical style that relies heavily on drums and instruments such as the *maracas* (rattles) and *marimbolas* (a keyboard made of bits of metal or wood that are plucked with the fingers or thumbs). The dance that accompanies rumba music is extremely expressive with a lot of exaggerated movement, particularly of the hips. The rumba also gained popularity through the 1935 musical film *Rumba*, which showcased this type of music and dance.

Rumba, however, was not the only Latino music and dance style that gained greater recognition in the United States through film. Throughout the 1930s and 1940s, moving pictures became more accessible and popular. One of the great legacies of this era of filmmaking was the American Western. Mexican culture was rarely portrayed accurately on screen, but

A Puerto Rican dance couple

Traditional Mexican musicians

it was through these cowboy films that many Americans got their first sampling of *mariachi* music.

Mariachi was originally working-class music from Mexico. Mariachi bands wore worker's clothes and traveled for miles. Mariachi is a blend of Spanish and *indigenous* music, combining five-string guitars called *vihuelas*, small thick-bodied guitars called *guitarrons*, violins, Spanish (six-string *acoustic*) guitars, basses, harps, and trumpets. The songs are usually about Mexican folktales, history, or romantic topics like love or lost heroes. Mariachi music has no percussion, but in the most common form of mariachi dance, *zapateado*, dancers use their shoes to beat out quick rhythms. These dances are so fast and vigorous that they even cause damage to the floor! Today most mariachi bands dress in

In Mexico, it is customary that only men play in mariachi bands, but many mariachi bands in the United States have women musicians too. In addition to movies, mariachi music also broke through thanks to the American singing group the Gumm Sisters, whose first musical hit was the mariachi classic "La Cucaracha" (in English, "La Cucaracha" means "The Cockroach").

the traditional Mexican *charro* suit, which is usually black with silver trim and buttons. Nevertheless, mariachi bands remain known for their hardworking ways.

In the 1940s a number of new Latin influences came to United States. *Samba*, which many American musicians had flirted with for years, finally made major inroads. The samba emerged from a combination of West African, Portuguese, and Native influences and is strongly associated with the celebration of *Carnival*. The dance had always been, and remains today, a symbol of rebelliousness in Brazil. In the United States, the dance and music were adapted to the ballroom where they became particularly popular. Nevertheless, the samba is still all about fun and can be performed to a variety of different types of music, which is part of the reason it remains popular today. It came to America thanks in large part to the "Brazilian Bombshell," Carmen Miranda. Miranda was a very talented

indigenous: something that is native to, or comes from, a given area. Native Americans, for example, are indigenous to America.

acoustic: relating to an instrument that is not amplified electronically.

Carnival: a large public festival with parades, costumes, music, and dancing held each year in Brazil.

Cuban musicians

singer, but today she is also remembered for her acting roles and her peculiar hats, which were piled high with fresh fruit.

At about the same time, *mambo* became extremely popular through a movement led by Pérez Prado, a Cuban bandleader also known as "the Mambo King." The mambo is a Haitian and Cuban form of music and dance that gets its name from a type of drum. Interestingly, the word mambo also means "conversation with the gods." In fact, in Haiti the word mambo refers to a *Voodoo* priestess. The music itself is a mix of mostly African rhythms with *swing* music, which gives mambo a big-band sound with strong drumming. The dance that accompanies this music ranges from fairly relaxed to highly acrobatic. It is not an easy dance to master, and for that reason became a favorite style for dance competitions in New York ballrooms in the 1950s. Today, typical mambo involves a lot of hip movement and sensual swaying to the music. You may have heard of Lou Bega's 2001 hit song "Mambo No. 5," which is a good example of the swinging sounds of mambo. Prado would also later be recognized for introducing another Cuban dance, the *cha cha cha* (better known today as the *cha cha*), which some regard as a high-speed version of the mambo.

Dancing to Cuban music

Another musician who was crowned as a "King of Mambo" in the 1940s and 1950s was Tito Puente, a New Yorker of Puerto Rican descent. Puente's career spanned half a century. In that time he recorded over one hundred albums, collected five Grammy Awards, and became a legend of American music.

In addition to the samba and mambo, the *calypso* also emerged as a force in the forties. This lively, cheerful music got its start in the Caribbean islands of Trinidad and Tobago, but it soon spread to its neighboring countries and to the American mainland. Calypso songs are often witty or funny, poking fun at political figures, life, or society in general. Like many musical styles with heavy African influences, calypso is very rhythm oriented with lots of beats from drums and percussion sticks. The singing in calypso often relies on a call-and-response technique in which a lead singer sings out a word or phrase and backup

Voodoo: a religion practiced in the Caribbean area, especially Haiti, that combines elements of Roman Catholicism and Native beliefs, and involves magic and communication with ancestors.

swing: a style of jazz and dance popular in the 1930s that relied on a big-band sound.

49

Steel drums are not African, as many people think, but developed in the Caribbean where poor musicians would beat on discarded oil drums left behind by trade ships visiting the island. One of the most famous calypso songs, and one that uses both steel drums and the call-and-response technique, is Harry Belafonte's "Banana Boat Song." You probably know it by its chorus lyric: "Day-O," featured prominently in the film *Beetlejuice*.

singers or the audience repeat the phrase or respond with another phrase. The steel drum features prominently in many calypso songs, giving the music a distinctly Caribbean sound.

There are two main kinds of dance that go along with calypso: carnival and ballroom. The carnival style of calypso is a free-spirited street dance. Sometimes called jump-dancing, it is often performed at celebrations or social events and can be danced solo, in pairs, or in large groups. The ballroom style, which is danced in couples, is more formal.

In 1944, one of the most popular singing groups in America, the Andrews Sisters, performed their rendition of a calypso song called "Rum and Coca Cola." Although it was somewhat removed from its Caribbean roots, the result of its success created a sudden interest in calypso and Caribbean sounds. Calypso continued to be played and danced to throughout the 1940s and 1950s.

Like calypso, the *conga*, a type of music and dance that comes from the island of Cuba, has strong African influences and relies on rhythms and beats. In fact, the conga gets its name from the African conga drum, which is popularly used to create the dance's beat.

The conga can be performed in two different ways. One, of course, is the famous conga line, in which people dance with their hands on the hips of the person in front of them, take three steps, and then kick in time to the music. People have long loved the conga because anyone can do it, it's easy to learn, and it's great fun in groups. A more complicated version of the conga can also be performed by couples with one partner facing the other.

Another Latino dance style Americans fell in love with for its simplicity is *merengue*. Two slightly different versions of this dance emerged from the island of Hispaniola (the dance is called *merengue* in the Dominican Republic and *meringue* in Haiti). A free-flowing dance, merengue is a favorite for parties and casual events. There is, however, a more complicated ballroom form in which partners hold hands and circle each other in a limping kind of movement. They may twist themselves into different kinds of handholds, move in figure-eights, or dance all around the room.

Like the dance, merengue music comes in many different forms. The traditional folk style relies on instruments like accordions, scrapers (called *guayanos*), and a double-sided drum called a *tambora*, which is beaten by hand and with a stick. More recent popular styles use a broad range of instruments, particularly big band instruments including trumpets, trombones, and saxophones.

The Birth of Jazz and Rock and Roll

In the 1950s, Latino sounds influenced another musical style: jazz. Some of the most famous jazz performers of all time, including jazz legend Dizzy Gillespie, decided to experiment with Latino sounds. The result of work from Gillespie and other artists who also incorporated these new sounds was to give Latin rhythms a permanent home in jazz

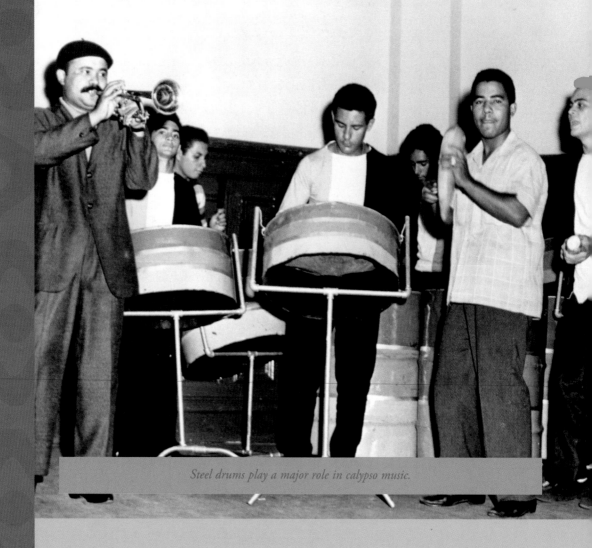

Steel drums play a major role in calypso music.

and pop music and to spawn an entirely new genre known today simply as Latin jazz.

In the 1950s and 1960s, the world saw the emergence of another kind of music that would soon dominate the airwaves: rock and roll. With America and Britain leading the way, electric guitars and catchy lyrics took over the charts. Among the most famous of the early rock and rollers was a Mexican American named Ritchie Valens. Very few songs in the 1950s were as popular as Valens's "La Bamba." This song was actually an adaptation of a traditional Mexican wedding song, and along with his other hit, "Donna," made him the first Latino rock and roll star.

The rock and roll sound pioneered by Valens soon found its way to Texas. There, itchie Valens met a tragic end in 1959. Just seventeen years old, he died when a plane carrying himself and fellow rock stars Buddy Holly and J. P. (the Big Bopper) Richardson crashed in a cornfield near Storm Lake, Iowa. Years later, rock and roller Don McLean's ballad "American Pie" (a version of which was recently recorded by Madonna) was inspired by the deaths of Valens, Holly, and Richardson. The lyric "the day the music died" refers to February 3, 1959—the date of the plane crash.

Tejanos, a group of people of Mexican descent, were using electric guitars and drums in their traditional music to create a whole new Latino sound. Their music, which can be called either Tejano or Tex-Mex, is an interesting mix of Mexican and European styles, particularly German ones. It has evolved and changed a lot over the years, incorporating strong jazz and rock influences, and it can even have a country music sound as well. The evolution of Tejano continued throughout the 1970s and 1980s with bands like La Familia and The Latin Breed. The 1990s saw a real explosion of popularity following the tragic death of star singer Selena Quintanilla.

Perhaps the biggest event in Latino music in the 1960s and 1970s, however, was the emergence of *salsa* music, which erupted from the Latino communities of New York City.

defecting: leaving the country of birth and refusing to return, often for political reasons.

Tito Puente at the Palladium, Home of the Mambo, in NYC

Today, salsa remains the dominant form of Latino music and dance in the United States. The word salsa simply means hot sauce, but a definition of salsa music is much harder to come by. Salsa incorporates sounds from many Latino styles and is most heavily influenced by the mambo.

There is no one style of salsa. Generally speaking, salsa's roots go back to the blending of African and Cuban musical styles with Puerto Rican influences and a touch of jazz. The vocals are often a combination of Spanish and English.

Cuban-born Celia Cruz is one of the most famous salsa singers of all time. After *defecting* from Cuba, she made a name for herself in America. She performed at New York's Carnegie Hall and went on to record more than twenty gold albums (a gold album is one that sells at least half a million copies). In that time she worked with Tito Puente and collaborated with Willie Colon, another famous New York musician with a Puerto Rican background. Cruz later joined a group of salsa musicians called the Fania All-Stars and brought her zesty music to the world. Artists like La India continued popularizing salsa throughout the 1980s, and today it remains enormously influential in most popular genres of American music, particularly jazz and dance.

As a result of the heavy influence of salsa on the American music industry, Latino singers and songwriters were instrumental in the creation of a broad array of dance music we now simply know as pop music. Cuban singer Gloria Estefan, who emerged in the mid-1980s, is one of the most famous innovators of pop and brought a distinctly Latino sound to her work. The 1980s also saw the emergence of one of the first boy bands, Menudo, which was made up of a group of young Latino singers and dancers.

A Puerto Rican rumbero

Latino Music Today

hat we know as Latin music today is often a pop-rock blend of Latino styles that have been in the United States for decades. Many cultures blended to create the unique sounds of Latin America. This cultural blending has continued in the United States, as artists from all walks of life choose to incorporate influences like tango, mambo, or rumba into their work. Latino music has been so influential in the United States that many artists who are not Latino have Latino sounds in their songs. Similarly, many Latino artists use more "American" sounds in their work.

Today, Latinos are a force in any genre of music you could mention. Rock and roll artists like Los Lobos and Carlos Santana are very popular. Joe King and Las Coronas have made their mark in punk rock. Johnny Rodriguez is a country music star, and Cypress Hill and Big Pun have had successful careers in rap. And, of course, Latinos continue to power Latin jazz and traditional styles of Latin music throughout the United States. The most famous Latino musicians, however, fall into the vague categories of pop, dance, or salsa. Ricky Martin (who got his start with Menudo), Jennifer Lopez, Marc Anthony, Shakira, and Christina Aguilera are just some of the more famous Latino names in the world of music. The degree to which each of them relies on traditional Latino sounds varies widely, but this is not surprising as the border between Latino and American music is now very fuzzy.

The difficulty in dividing American and Latino culture into totally separate entities is a theme that comes up again and again in the world of art. The blending of these two identities is something many Latinos have seen fit to write about. Just as music and dance have been important artistic mediums for Latinos in the United States, literature has also been an influential mode for artistic and cultural expression.

Latino influence in music and dance hasn't been limited to popular culture. It has also been important in more formal realms. In the 1940s and 1950s, Mexican-born dancer and choreographer Jose Límon established the Límon Dance Company in New York and became an enormous and groundbreaking influence in modern dance. Límon received numerous awards for his choreography and taught at the Julliard School of Dance, bringing Latino elements into the most prestigious dance school in the country and into the mainstream of American dance.

Habla Español

danza (dahn-sah): dance

musica (moo-see-cah): music

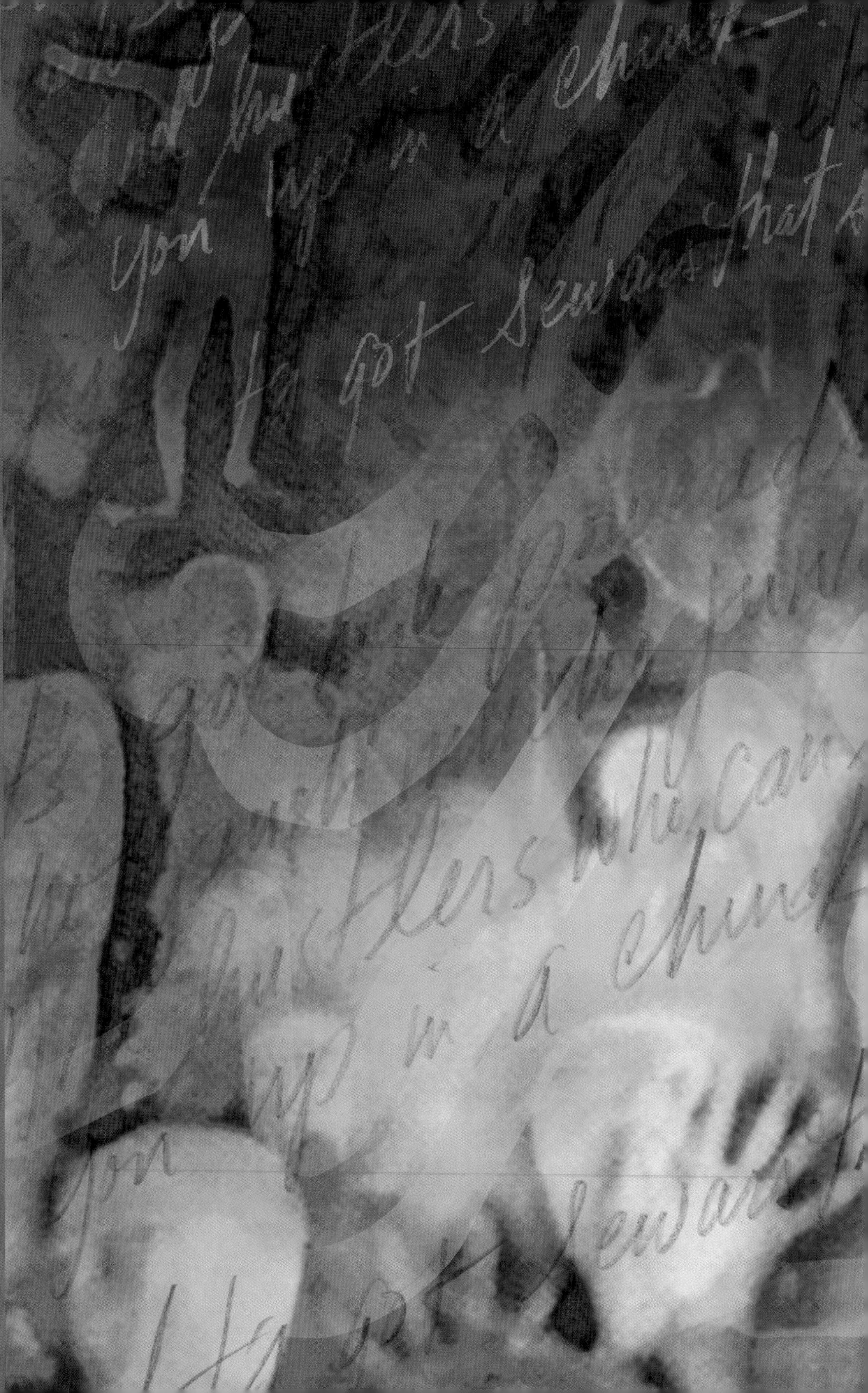

Stories and Poems: Latino Writers Capture Culture with Words

In the 1930s, the time of the Great Depression, growing up in Spanish Harlem meant growing up in a world where drugs, gangs, racism, and violence were just a step outside your door. It was a place where work was hard to come by in a time when money was scarce and hope was in short supply. The houses and apartments of *El Barrio* were run down, and many were too small for the families who lived in them. It was a hard place to live and a difficult place from which to escape. If you were going to get by at all in El Barrio, you had to be tough.

El Barrio: in Spanish, barrio means "neighborhood." Many Latinos refer to the neighborhood in which they grew up as El Barrio, or The Neighborhood.

59

Hispanic graffiti

Poverty is a way of life for many Latinos.

Born to Cuban and Puerto Rican parents, Piri Thomas grew up in Spanish Harlem. Growing up in an island of Latino culture surrounded by a sea of Anglos, Piri soon learned that the world he lived in was divided by lines: rich and poor, American and immigrant, English and Spanish, white and nonwhite. He also discovered that which side of the line one fell on determined many important things about what one could and couldn't do.

At twenty-two years old, Piri made a decision that changed his life. He and two friends decided to rob a nightclub. Piri's job was to guard the door. The robbery did not go well; the police showed up, and a gunfight broke out. One of the officers shot Piri in the chest. The bullet just barely missed his heart, coming within half an inch of killing him. Piri fired back, and the police officer was hit and badly wounded. While both men escaped with their lives, Piri spent the next seven years behind bars.

Prison gave Piri time to reflect on life, his identity, and the society in which he lived. He started focusing on the problems he faced, the people he loved, and how the world could and should change for the better. Soon, ideas were forming in his mind, and he began coming to terms with himself. As he did, he began writing.

Latino Writers in the United States

iri Thomas emerged from prison with a new and bold understanding of life. Where he had once focused on the

Piri Thomas

pain and the poverty that seemed to come with being Latino in America, he began to focus on the love and the proud history that people in his community shared. The barrio of his past had nearly led to his destruction, and he was determined to help create a new environment that would prevent others from following the same path.

Today, Piri Thomas is recognized as one of the most influential Latino writers in U.S. history. His words have found their way into the hearts of America's Puerto Rican communities, and his stories have brought these communities into the American consciousness. He has become a symbol of the emerging Nuyorican culture and a source of pride and inspiration. Thomas's 1967 book, *Down These Mean Streets*, which tells about his life,

Puerto Ricans in New York City

is now an American classic. This book helped Americans to understand a culture that was largely ignored and illuminated the struggles many Latinos face.

Like Piri Thomas, many Latino writers in America found their voices during the 1960s and 1970s. It was a time of social revolution and political upheaval in the United States, and the civil rights movement was bringing some of the most *disaffected* communities in the country together to demand change. People who had lived on the edges of society were now building new cultural identities and showing pride in their backgrounds in a way they had never done before. Just like African American communities, with leaders like Martin Luther King Jr. and Malcolm X, Latino communities were coming together and speaking out. It was during these two decades that the Chicanos and

Nuyoricans really started to establish themselves, and many in these communities chose to express themselves through art, with poetry and *prose* becoming particularly powerful ways of communicating new cultural ideas and values.

Not long after *Down These Mean Streets* was published, other writers who would be embraced by the Nuyorican movement, like Nicholasa Mohr and Edward Rivera, started to emerge. Their works became rallying points as their writings about cultural pride and identity gave people hope and inspired them to create change. For some, the split in the Puerto Rican identity—belonging to the Puerto Rican homeland or the adopted American home—was healed as the Nuyorican identity embraced both aspects and fused them into something new, something they could be proud of. The message of Nuyorican writers *transcended* borders and was communicated to Latinos of various backgrounds throughout the United States. It is a message that is still vibrant today.

disaffected: a feeling of distress or discontent, often resulting from being neglected or ignored.

prose: literature that is in the form of ordinary speech, unlike poetry, which has set rhythms and rhymes, or is different from how a person would normally speak.

transcended: crossed or went beyond a border or limit.

he base for Nuyorican writers remains in New York City, especially at the Nuyorican Poetry Café. There, the work of influential Nuyorican poets like Jorge Brandon and Miguel Algarín are read, along with new and emerging voices from the barrios of America.

Chicano street artists give expression to some of the same themes as Chicano authors.

The East Coast experiences of Nuyoricans of the kind laid out by Piri Thomas were mirrored on the opposite side of the country by Chicano writers. Just like the Puerto Ricans of New York, the Mexican Americans of California and the American Southwest were struggling to find their place. They were mostly poor, and felt pushed aside and rejected by the mainstream of Anglo-America. This was until the emergence of Chicanismo, and a return to pride in the Mexican identity and culture (see chapter 2 for a review of Chicanismo).

In 1972, writer Rudolfo Anaya published what is probably the best-selling Chicano novel of all time, *Bless Me, Ultima*. At about the same time, Rodolfo "Corky" Gonzales published the most famous Chicano poem, making 1972 a banner year for Chicano literature. Gonzales's poem, "I am Joaquín," could have been adopted by many of America's minority communities to describe their struggle to retain their cultures against the powerful influences of American society.

These two works, like a lot of Chicano writing, were personal and focused strongly on concepts of family, community, history, and the dilemma of whether to define one's iden-

Rudolfo Anaya

tity as more Mexican or more American. There are many Chicano books that portray issues important to the larger Chicano community through the *autobiographical* experiences of the writer. Much of Chicano writing also deals with feelings of oppression in the Chicano community, much of which is blamed on the Anglo schools and institutions that have been so hard for people of Mexican descent to access.

In recent years, Chicano writing has branched out in style and content. It has also started to come from more diverse sources, with women in particular becoming more influential. Some of the most widely acclaimed Chicano writers are women. Chicana authors like Sandra Cisneros, Lorna Dee Cervantes, Kathleen Alcalá, and Julia Alvarez have all made major contributions to Chicano culture and have been crucial in establishing a female perspective on the Chicano movement. They have also

autobiographical: told or written by a writer about herself.

Chicano authors express the beauty and patterns of their world.

Nobel Prize for Literature: perhaps the most prestigious prize any writer can win. Only one person in the entire world is chosen as a winner each year. There are also Nobel Prizes in other areas like physics, medicine, and chemistry.

ablo Neruda, Gabriel García Márquez, and Octavio Paz have all won the *Nobel Prize for Literature* honoring their work.

Oscar Hijuelos

attracted a broad new audience to Chicano literature, spreading knowledge about their culture and achieving commercial success for themselves and other Latino writers in the process.

In addition to Chicano and Nuyorican writers, Cuban Americans have asserted their culture through books and poems as well. The Cuban American community in the United States has its own unique story, especially because Cuban Americans are in a unique relationship with their homeland, the island of Cuba. Many of the Cuban people living in America today believed that they would only be staying in the United States until Cuba's leader, Fidel Castro, and his *Communist* Party were overthrown. However, decades have dragged on since Castro first came to power in 1959, and many Cuban Americans now wonder if they will ever again see their island home. Despite the passing years, the Cuban American community maintains close ties with the island, is extremely politically active, and continues to exert a profound affect on American foreign policy toward Cuba. The Cuban American community retains a strong sense of pride in their roots and has made great efforts to keep their culture alive, particularly in Florida, which has a large Cuban American population.

Famous Cuban American writers whose works center on Cuban culture include poets like Lourdes Gil and novelists such as Gustavo Pérez Firmat, Margarita Engle, and Jose Yglesias. One Cuban American novelist in particular, Oscar Hijuelos, has had enormous success, winning a *Pulitzer Prize* for his work *The Mambo Kings Play Songs of Love.*

Classics of Latino Literature

In addition to those writers who achieved success from within the United States, there are also a large number of Latin American people who have influenced America from beyond its borders. Among the earliest was a woman named Sor Juana Inés de la Cruz.

Sor Juana was a Catholic nun who lived in Mexico in the late seventeenth century. When she was a child, girls were not allowed to go to school, so most of Sor Juana's learning was done in her grandfather's library. By the time she was a young woman, she was known as a prodigy, a genius with a remarkable understanding of the world. She penned several plays, poems, and essays and believed strongly that women had as much of a right to education as did men. Sor Juana's opinions frequently landed her in hot water with the Catholic Church, which did not advocate for women's equality. She has since become a *feminist icon*, and her essay, *Reply to Sor Philothea*, is an excellent example of feminist writing and philosophy.

As time has passed, Latino writers have become increasingly influential in the United States and around the world. Mexico

Communist: people who follow a philosophy that was dominant in the former Soviet Union, and which involves government or common control of the economy. It is contrasted with America's free-market system, which allows anyone to set up a business and to operate it for profit.

Pulitzer Prize: a prestigious American award that recognizes excellent writing in a number of different categories.

feminist: belonging to the philosophy of feminism, which emphasizes the rights of women and equality between genders.

icon: a visible symbol.

Children in New York City barrios live the rhythms of Latino life, the same rhythms that Hispanic authors capture in their work.

has produced brilliant authors such as Carlos Fuentes, who wrote *The Death of Artemio Cruz* and continues to sell well internationally, and Octavio Paz, whose book *The Labyrinth of Solitude* remains one of the most influential works describing Mexican identity. Chilé brought the world writers like Isabel Allende, whose book *The House of the Spirits* was an international bestseller in the early 1980s, and poet Pablo Neruda, who was a powerful and controversial voice for *Marxism*. Argentina's Jorge Luis Borges is a master of fantasy and *surrealist* literature whose work in the early part of the twentieth century remains influential today. The works of Brazil's Jorge Amado have been translated into almost fifty languages and have sold more than twenty million copies worldwide. José Martí, a Cuban writer who spent many years writing in the United States at the turn of the twentieth century, was a strong voice for Cuban independence. Colombia's Gabriel García Márquez's book *One Hundred Years of Solitude* had to be reprinted multiple times in the United States because of its enormous popularity.

Latino dance, music, and literature have had an incredible impact on arts and culture in the United States, but they are certainly not the only art forms that have been influential. Latino visual arts have also been embraced in the United States, both for their beauty and for the ideas they communicate.

Marxism: a political and economic theory based on the ideas of Karl Marx and Friedrich Engels which claimed that class struggle was the primary cause of social change in Western societies.

surrealist: someone who created art and literature in the manner of the early twentieth-century movement called surrealism, which represented the subconscious mind by using fantastic imagery and ironic placement of objects.

Habla Español

cuentos (kwane-toes): stories

palabras (pah-lah-bras): words

poemas (poe-ae-mahs): poems

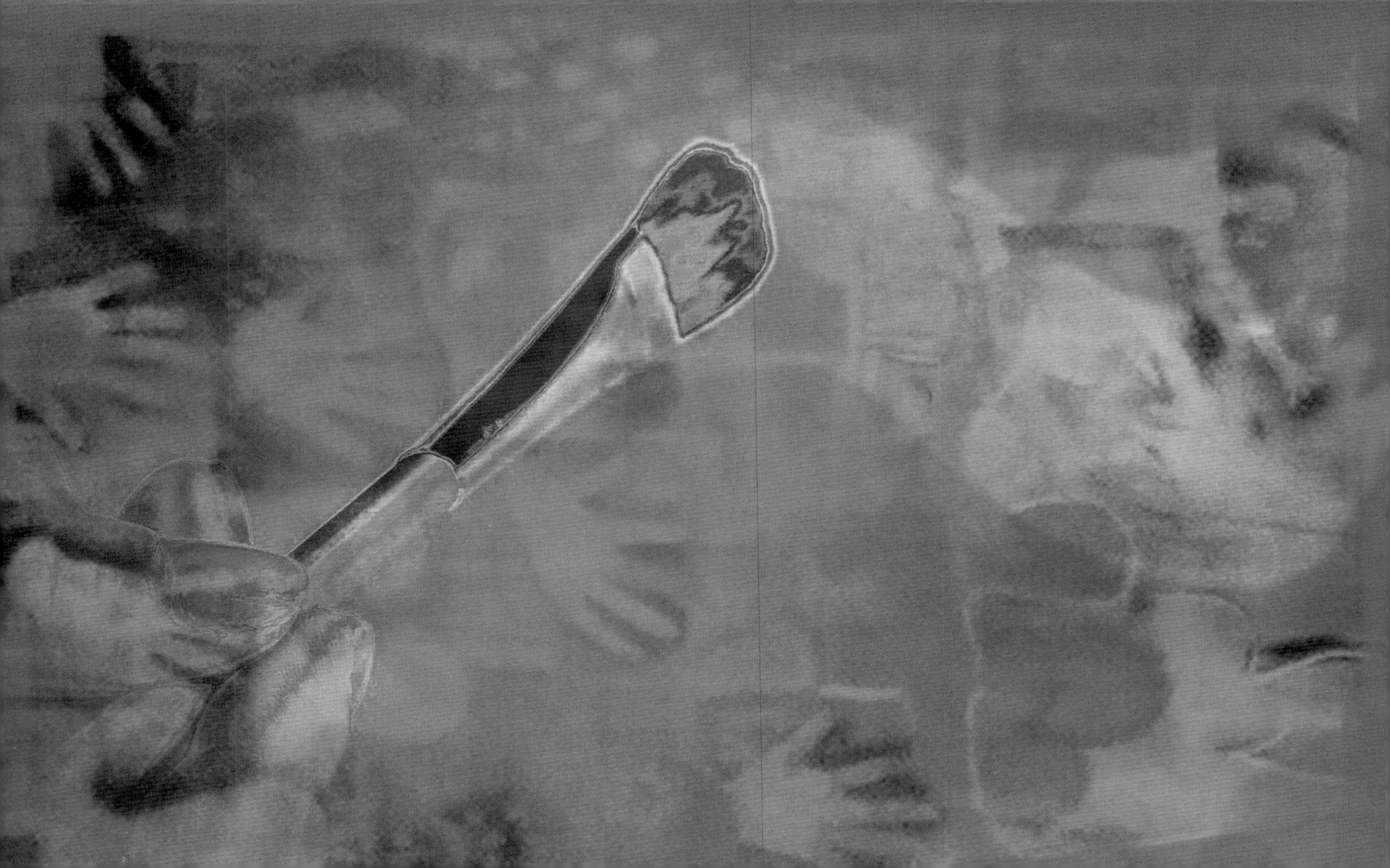

5

Painting Change: Latino Imagery and Its Impact in the United States

People from your parents' generation may know an actor named Cheech Marin as one half of the comedy act Cheech and Chong. Back in the early 1970s they made record albums with comedy routines about smoking pot and other "scandalous" things. In 1978, Cheech and Chong went to the movie screens with their film *Up in Smoke*. Over the years, however, Marin mellowed; maybe you can only make so many jokes about smoking weed. Since then, he has been in films including *Spy Kids* and *Desperado*. He also added his voice to one of the characters in Disney's *Lion King* cartoon.

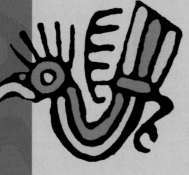

Then in 2001, Marin surprised the world by heading in an entirely different direction. It turns out that Marin is an avid collector of Latino art. He organized Hispanic artists and collectors to create the largest single show of Latino art—and put it on the road. He said he wanted to open people's eyes to the world of Chicano art. "People can't appreciate it until they know about it, and that's what this whole tour is about," he says.

When it comes to Latino art, there is plenty to learn about and appreciate. There are Hispanic artists famous and anonymous, sacred and scandalous, abstract and realistic, comforting and provocative.

Los Viejos (the Old Ones)

oday's Latino artists find inspiration from their ancient ancestors, both Indian and European. The pre-Columbian Indians of Mexico, Central America, and South America were highly sophisticated artists. The Olmecs, for example, left behind enormous heads with bold features, reminiscent of the famous statues of Easter Island. The Mayans were known particularly for their pottery, which often incorporated multicolored pictures or writing. They also created intricate stone sculptures, colorful woven fabrics, and large murals depicting important stories. The Aztecs also used art to tell stories and created limestone carvings representing gods or animals. Aztec architectural styles, characterized by geometric patterns, have been incorporated into modern buildings, particularly in Mexico. The bright

An Aztec carving

geometric styles of Aztec painting continue to inspire modern Latino painters. Murals created by young men with spray cans in Pilsen, Illinois, or Highland Park, California, incorporate Aztec designs and themes.

The Incas, like the Maya and Aztecs, were also skilled artists and architects, but they tended to use metal as much as stone. Their intricate sculptures and jewelry were often made from gold and precious stones and like most Incan art, were created with a high degree of precision and attention to detail. The artists of these great civilizations created works of lasting beauty that centuries later still inspire modern Latino artists. Although these civilizations were brutally conquered, their art could not be destroyed and continues to survive and influence Latino culture today.

When they crossed the ocean, the Spanish brought their own tradition of fine art with them. At the time of the conquest, the new style of painting was called Mannerism. Mannerist paintings lack a clearly defined focal point; figures crowd the space and sometimes seem to pop out of it. Bodies are exaggerated and contorted, not realistic. The most famous Spanish Mannerist was Doménikos Theotokópoulos, commonly known as El Greco. He painted religious themes that were rendered more emotional by dramatic use of colors and exaggerated proportions. The influence of Mannerist artists can be seen in the later paintings of Diego Rivera, Frida Kahlo, and murals on city walls throughout the United States today.

Anonymous *santeros* of the colonial Southwest have also left their mark on Latino art. A santero is an artist who carves wooden statues of *santos* (saints). These santos were not made for commercial purposes or mere decoration. They were intended to focus the prayers of Catholic believers, directing them from the image to a supernatural reality. Today, these unnamed

Latino santos

Santos depicting various saints

artists who worked in New Mexico, California, Texas, and Arizona are highly regarded. Their work was once a means of spiritual devotion, used often by poor people. Popular subjects are *San Francisco* (Saint Francis), the *Virgen de Guadalupe*, and *San Miguel* (Saint Michael the Archangel). These were simple figures, made with little more than a piece of pine and a sharp knife, but the santeros were able to carve images with considerable expression. Today, santos are highly sought by collectors and continue to inspire contemporary Latino artists.

José Guadalupe Posada

hen Posada died in 1913, few people had heard of him, even in his native Mexico. Yet since then he has influenced art around the world. His influence can particularly be seen among Latinos in California and Texas, where the popular art today often incorporates Posada's *calaveras* (skeletons).

Posada was a poor man for his entire life. He worked for little pay for penny newspapers, making images by engraving metal plates. The plates were smeared with ink and used in newspaper presses. This process produces images with strong black and white lines.

Posada is famous for his subject matter—skeletons, comically dressed to resemble the people he saw around him. One is a woman wearing a fancy hat, another is a cowboy riding his horse. He portrayed peasants dancing and intellectuals writing and talking—all as skeletons. Posada's calaveras had ancient roots. The Aztec Indians often portrayed skeletal figures in their art.

Posada lived during some of Mexico's most violent years. As a boy, he witnessed the horrors of the Mexican-French War, and as an older man he was troubled by the brutality of the Mexican Revolution. The skeletons he drew were his way of mocking death. Their comical demeanor helped Mexicans to face hard times with a sense of humor.

Today, skeletons are also a symbol of the *Dia de Los Muertos*, an annual holiday celebrated in Mexico and in the United States (we will discuss this holiday in more detail in chapter 6). Comical skeletons are a common theme in Latino art, seen on

One of Posada's cheerful skeletons

postmodernism: an artistic and architectural movement showing a return to more classical and traditional subjects and techniques than what had been used in the modernist movement.

cubism: an early twentieth-century art movement that emphasized geometric shapes seen from several angles.

t-shirts, silkscreen prints, and expensive paintings by well-known artists such as George Yepes. Countless Latino murals in American urban centers include calaveras as subject matter. Demonstrating the way symbols travel far from their roots, skeletons are the ever-popular symbol for the rock band Grateful Dead. Few artists are as influential, yet as unrecognized by name as José Guadalupe Posada.

Diego Rivera

uring the 1930s, Diego Rivera, José Clemente Orozco, and David Alfaro Sisqueiros established the Muralismo movement. They have become known as *Las Tres Grandes* (the Three Greats). All three began working in Mexico, but they also painted murals commissioned by major cities throughout the United States. As a result, they continue to influence the world of art. They especially inspire Latino artists—both muralists and those who work with canvas. Prints taken from Rivera's murals are still very popular and adorn innumerable homes and offices owned by both Hispanics and Anglos.

Diego Rivera was one of the greatest artists of the twentieth century. He was born in Guanajuato, Mexico, in 1886, and when he was six years old, his family moved to Mexico City. He studied in the San Carlos Academy and worked with José Guadalupe Posada. Later, he traveled to Europe, where he was influenced by the art schools of *postmodernism* and *cubism*. In Italy, he took in the great painters of the Renaissance. Rivera's paintings use earth-tone colors, giving a natural, organic feel. He gave new meaning to themes and designs from

Don Quijote as portrayed by Posada

pre-Columbian Indian art by placing them in new contexts. His favorite subjects were
Mexico's history, the earth, farmers, laborers, and flowers.

In the 1930s, Rivera was paid to paint murals in major cities of the United States. He
was asked to paint large murals at the Detroit Art Institute and at the Rockefeller Center
in New York, where his fresco *Hombre en la Encrucijada (Man at the Crossroads)*, was crit-
icized because it contained the image of Lenin, the Communist leader. The Rockefeller
Center destroyed his mural, but he painted another one like it in Mexico City.

Rivera was a nonconformist whose beliefs and behavior often got him in trouble.
Mexico City's Hotel del Prado refused to show a Rivera fresco that bore the words *"Díos
no existe"* (God does not exist).

polio: short for poliomyelitis, it is a viral disease that can cause weakness, paralysis, and death.

But the controversy Diego Rivera generated pales in comparison with the greatness of his art. His painting style influenced generations of artists after him. Scores of mural painters in the United States imitated his style of painting on the walls of public buildings. He also influenced the explosion of Hispanic mural painters from the 1960s through today.

Frida Kahlo

In the United States today, Frida Kahlo may be the best known of all Mexican artists, but in 1922, she was just a fifteen-year-old schoolgirl studying at the National Preparatory School in Mexico City. She had a very mixed background, with Jewish, German, Spanish, and Indian roots. Even as a young girl, Frida had strong beliefs and a fierce determination. Frida took up art at the age of seven, when she suffered a bout of *polio*. Her father bought her a paint set to keep her busy while she was ill. The polio left her right leg weak and underdeveloped, a condition that never got better, but it also left her with an interest in painting and an outlet for her ideas and emotions. After her illness, however, she had had little reason to do much painting and set her sights on other things, particularly having fun. She was known for joking around, playing pranks, and being mischievous. She also enjoyed wearing bright clothing and jewelry, much of which represented the Native cultures of Mexico.

One day something happened that got Frida thinking about art again: The famous artist Diego Rivera arrived at her school.

The Other Greats

iego Rivera is best known of Las Tres Grandes, but in the 1930s, his two companions—José Clemente Orozco and David Alfaro Siqueiros—were also very famous. Some of Orozco's best murals are in southern California and New York. Orozco's art is more abstract than Rivera's. While Rivera loved organic, curving lines, Orozco drew more geometric designs. Many of his paintings express his concern for liberation of the poor.

All three of the great muralists were concerned with radical social change, but David Alfaro Siqueiros's murals are even more radical than Rivera's and Orozco's. Siqueiros was exiled from Mexico in 1932, and he moved to the United States. In California, he was hired to paint a mural for the Old Pueblo section of downtown Los Angeles. His finished piece was called *America Tropical*. He used dark and somber colors, rather than the bright tones expected of a Mexican artist. The center of the piece showed an Indian crucified by an American eagle. There was such an outcry that the mural was painted over, and Siqueiros was deported. Siqueiros's paintings are jarring, powerful images. Looking at them, it is impossible not to feel the artist's rage for social injustice.

Frida Kahlo's studio in Mexico City

He was being paid to paint a mural in the school's auditorium. At thirty-six years old, Diego was much older than Frida. All the same, Frida took an immediate interest in him and tried to get his attention by playing pranks like stealing his lunch. Diego was engaged to be married, and Frida's efforts left her empty-handed—at least for the time being.

Diego finished his mural at the school and left to start work elsewhere in Mexico. With him gone, Frida turned her interest to other boys and to her studies. By the time she was eighteen, she dreamed of becoming a doctor. Her boyfriend, Alejandro, also wanted to go to medical school. They talked about their plans on the bus one day as it drove them to their hometown of Coyoacán. Frida had no idea that her life was about to change forever.

In a split second the bus was ripped apart as a trolley car slammed into its side. The passengers were thrown everywhere. People screamed and cried. Alejandro was injured, but he was conscious and set about looking for Frida in the wreckage. When he found her, she was fighting for her life. A metal pole had speared her abdomen. Vertebrae in her spine were broken, along with two of her ribs and her pelvis. Her polio-weakened leg was shattered.

Frida was taken to the hospital, and though she would live, her life for the next few

rida and Diego were part of a cultural movement known as *Mexicanidad*, which encouraged wearing traditional Mexican clothes and collecting folk art. Frida became famous for her traditional Mexican outfits. Mexicanidad also influenced her art. Her paintings reflect the influences of Colonial Spanish Mannerism and religious Mexican folk art.

months was full of suffering and pain. Her body was almost entirely covered by casts, and any movement was agony. She wrote letters to Alejandro, but he never wrote back. Just as she had done when she had been sick with polio, Frida turned to painting to pass the painful hours. When she finally healed and learned to walk again, she no longer wanted to become a doctor. She was an aspiring artist. She had other goals, too, among them to find Diego Rivera.

Frida found Diego at the Ministry of Education where he worked for the government. She had brought some of her art. She hoped Diego would give her his thoughts on whether she really could be an artist. Diego, now divorced, admired both the paintings and the strong woman who had created them. Diego and Frida had long conversations and discovered they shared many of the same beliefs and values. Soon they spent all their time together. Their love blossomed, and in 1929 they were married.

As she and Diego traveled about America, Frida's artwork went largely ignored. She felt as though she was living her life in her husband's shadow. She started to paint less and less and concentrated on supporting her husband in his work. She was proud of Diego, but she also felt lonely and unappreciated. She sometimes referred to her marriage as "the second accident in my life." She loved Rivera passionately, but he continually cheated on her. Rivera even had an affair with Kahlo's sister Christina. To get even, Frida had affairs also.

Frida's emotional pain was made worse by the physical pain and complications that still remained from the bus accident. She was hospitalized many times and had more than thirty surgeries. Frida's art reflects her pain, and it is perhaps this quality that later made her such an icon. In his autobiography, Rivera said, "Frida began work on a series of masterpieces which had no precedent in the history of art—paintings which exalted the feminine qualities of endurance of truth, reality, cruelty, and suffering. Never before had a woman put such agonized poetry on canvas as Frida did. . . ."

Frida continued to paint through her pain, but over time her health deteriorated. In 1953 her damaged right leg was amputated, and in 1954 she died at the age of forty-seven. Diego Rivera died just three years later.

Modern-Day Muralismo

In the 1970s, Chicano artists began painting walls and sides of businesses as a way of dramatizing their social concerns. It was also a statement that said, "This part of the city is Chicano space." Today, the great tradition of painting outdoor murals lives on more than ever. In any major American city (and some smaller ones, too) you can drive around admiring painted expressions of Latino pride. In some cities, like Los Angeles, California, or Pilsen, Illinois, you could do this all day.

A Mexican mural

Well-known artists whose canvas paintings sell for big bucks produce some of these murals. Anonymous artists paint others. Each mural tells a story. They combine elements of Aztec, Mexican, and U.S. culture. If you live near a city, get out and walk around. Take a close look at these amazing displays of talent. Some would make Diego Rivera proud.

As cities create more *ordinances*, murals also create controversy. A mural in a California city was ordered painted over because it portrayed a police officer as, literally, a pig, beating a person of color with his baton. Should cities censor art that is offensive or unsettling, or should artists be allowed to express themselves free of censorship? Some mu-

Dominican artist Jorge Sanchez displays his surrealist work.

rals have been destroyed because of zoning restrictions, even though storeowners and residents of the community requested a mural. People also disagree over what makes a mural "art." (Remember our discussion in chapter 1?) What is the difference between graffiti (generally considered undesirable) and urban art (highly esteemed)? Beauty may be in the eye of the beholder, but what goes and what stays on city walls often depends on the decisions of city governments.

exiled: unwillingly forced to leave the country of one's birth or residence.

New Expressions in Latino Art

In recent times, Latino artists have diversified their work enormously. There is constant innovation and experimentation in the world of art, and Latinos are no exception. Ana Mendieta, for example, who was *exiled* from her native Cuba in 1961, incorporates elements like fire, water, and earth into her work, and her imagery often deals with the joining of the female body with nature. Though it would be very hard to look at her work and describe it as Latino, it is an excellent example of how Latino artists can have an influence without restricting themselves to "traditional" Latino art. As is the case in most art forms, it can now be difficult to tell where the dividing lines between Latino and American are and to figure out who is influencing whom. It can also be hard to tell where culture ends and where the artist's individual personality begins.

Like Mendieta, Pepón Osorio is a Latino artist whose modern art incorporates a variety of materials. Born in Puerto Rico in 1955, Osorio was educated at the Universidad Inter-

The Aztec influence is obvious in this modern building.

Americana, the Herbert H. Lehman College in New York, and Columbia University. He also worked as a social worker in the Bronx, and his experiences influenced his art. "My principal commitment as an artist is to return art to the community," he says. A recent example is *Tina's House*, inspired by a family recovering from a devastating fire. The house—a tabletop-size art piece—tells the story of the fire. This art piece is traveling the country in a series of "home visits." A home visit invites a new family to live with the art-work for a period of at least one week, allowing the story of *Tina's House* to be told in many homes and environments. Today Pepón Osorio lives in Philadelphia.

On the other side of the country, painter and muralist George Yepes was named a "Treasure of Los Angeles" in 1997 by Mayor Richard Riordan. Born in Tijuana and raised in East Lost Angeles, Yepes experienced the street life of poverty and gang violence in his youth. Today he is a self-taught artist, influenced both by classical Renaissance painters and by the great Mexican muralists.

Yepes has painted social, historical, and sacred "canvases" ranging from churches to hospitals to album covers. Sean Penn and Madonna bought his painting titled *La Pistola y el Corazon* for a record-breaking sum in 1989. He has painted twenty-eight noted murals in Los Angeles, and his Academia de Arte Yepes students have painted twenty-one more. The Academia is a free mural-painting school. Yepes has taught nearly 1,500 low-income students over the last decade.

oday, many Latino artists have become icons of their home cultures. This is largely because they give a voice to the culture, history, religion, and politics of their home countries and provide a sense of national pride and identity to those who view their work. Many Latin American countries have gone through long periods of political unrest and many changes of government. Some scholars note that one of the major functions of Latin American art has been to act as a stable representation of the people, even when their worlds are undergoing big changes. In this way, Latino artists serve as a unifying force in their communities. Their art brings people together and reminds them of what their culture is all about even in times of uncertainty and change.

Habla Espanol

artista (ahr-tees-tah): artist

color (coe-lore): color

pinta (peen-tah): paint

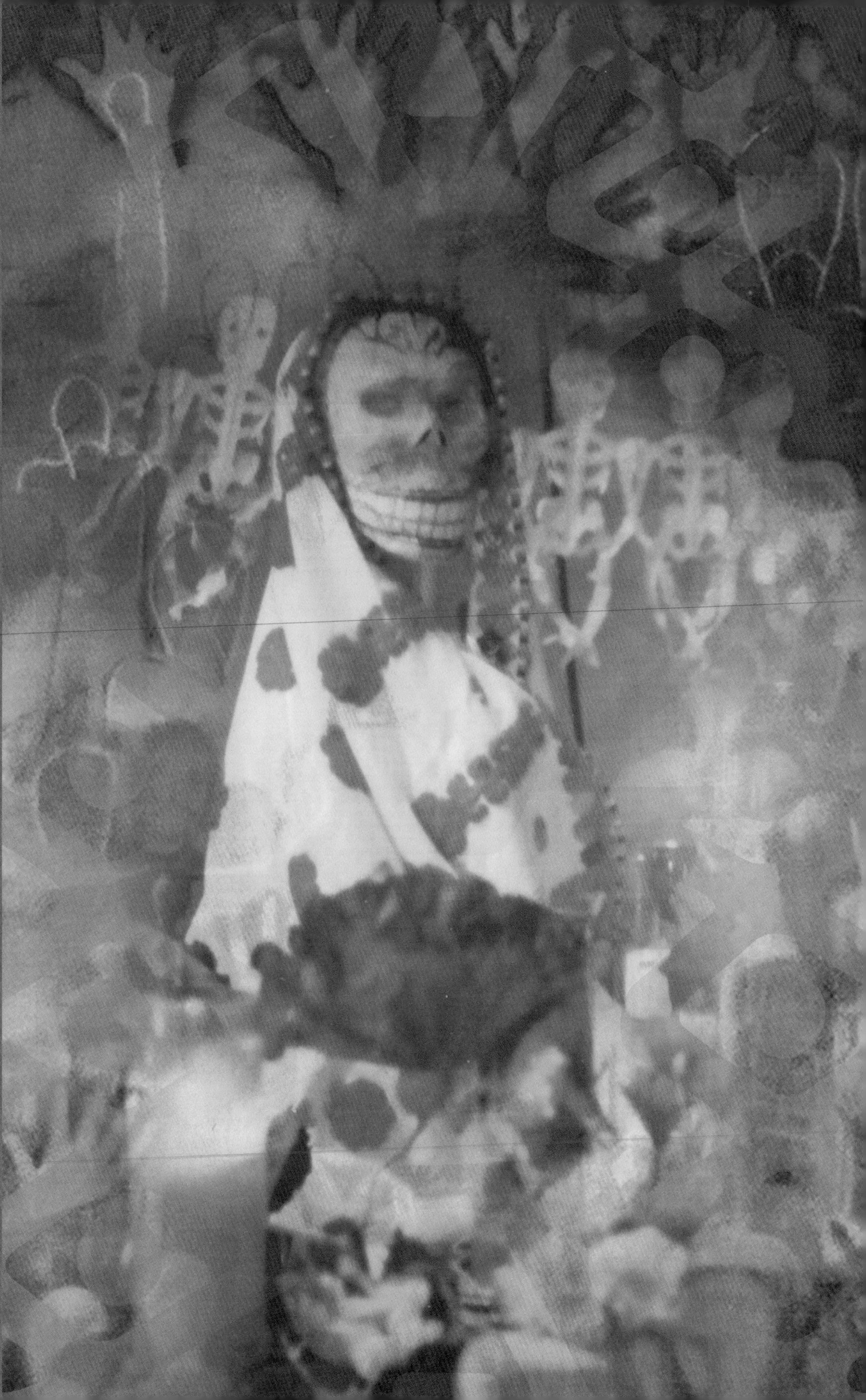

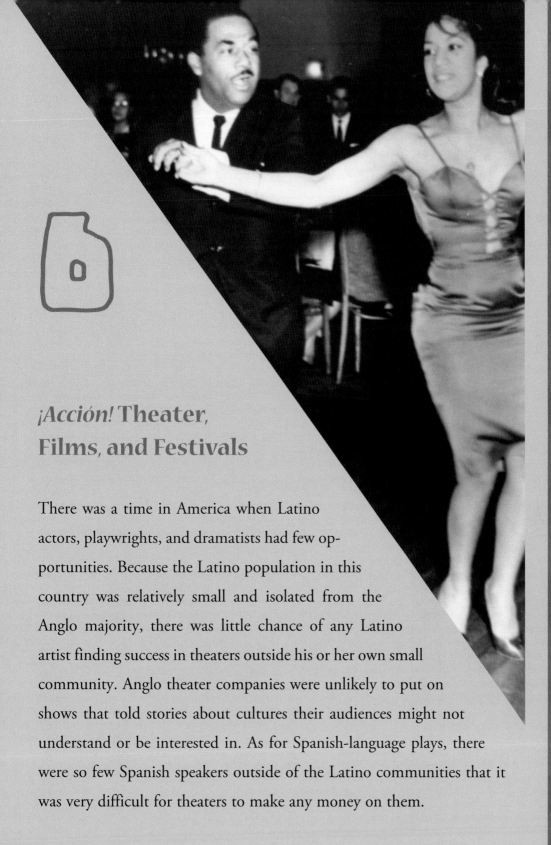

¡Acción! Theater, Films, and Festivals

There was a time in America when Latino actors, playwrights, and dramatists had few opportunities. Because the Latino population in this country was relatively small and isolated from the Anglo majority, there was little chance of any Latino artist finding success in theaters outside his or her own small community. Anglo theater companies were unlikely to put on shows that told stories about cultures their audiences might not understand or be interested in. As for Spanish-language plays, there were so few Spanish speakers outside of the Latino communities that it was very difficult for theaters to make any money on them.

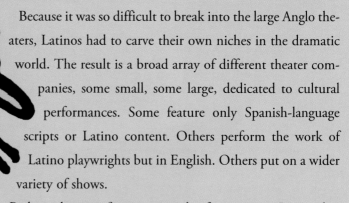

Because it was so difficult to break into the large Anglo theaters, Latinos had to carve their own niches in the dramatic world. The result is a broad array of different theater companies, some small, some large, dedicated to cultural performances. Some feature only Spanish-language scripts or Latino content. Others perform the work of Latino playwrights but in English. Others put on a wider variety of shows.

Perhaps the most famous example of a grassroots Latino theater company is El Teatro Campesino (roughly translated, this means "Farmer's Theater"). El Teatro was founded in 1965, shortly after César Chávez and the National Farm Workers Association went on strike in California (see chapter 2 for more information). The principal founder of El Teatro was Luis Valdez, a playwright and member of the San Francisco Mime Troupe. Valdez left the Troupe to join César Chávez and ended up creating El Teatro Campesino, which put on plays in farm fields to teach workers about their rights. All of the acting, scripting, and directing was performed by Mexican Americans, most of them farmworkers themselves. Soon, the theater took its act on the road to spread Chicano culture and raise political issues with broader audiences.

Farmworkers learn about their rights from El Teatro Campesino.

El Teatro Campesino spread beyond California. By 1980 it had received national and even international recognition and earned numerous awards for its performances and political message. El Teatro set the stage for the emergence of other Latino theater companies, and each of these brought its own voice and style. Over time, Latino theater companies have diversified their content and their message. Today there is a rich array of Latino theater in the United States, much of it based in either Los Angeles or New York.

In the 1950s and '60s, television and movies seldom portrayed ordinary Latinos like these.

Latinos in Film

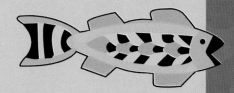

ust as they have been underrepresented on stage, Latinos have also been under-represented in American films and TV programs. There have been fewer roles for Latino actors and fewer films about Latino culture. From the "bad guys" in old Western movies, to the drug pushers in more recent gangster movies, when Latinos *are* portrayed on screen, their characters are often based on stereotypes. Even today, many movies and television

shows, rather than exploring what it means to be Latino, simply use Latino characters to fill stereotypical roles, especially ones associated with crime and poverty. Movies such as *Scarface*, which is about Cuban American gang life, may cause American audiences to see Latinos in a negative way without really understanding Latino culture at all. Fortunately, there are many people working to change these representations in the American popular media.

Latinos are becoming more influential in the movie and television industries, and the Latino population in America is growing, making it more likely that films with Latino cultural content are going to be successful. Twenty years ago, there were very few Latinos who rose to fame on the screen. People who did include Desi Arnaz, who played Ricky Ricardo on *I Love Lucy*, and Ricardo Montalban, who starred on *Fantasy Island*. Today, however, many more Latinos are making their mark either acting, writing, or directing, and there are many more films being produced that focus on Latino culture.

Many Latinos who have made it to the screen are people who were already famous in other artistic fields before entering into acting. Brazilian singer Carmen Miranda is an early example of a musician turned actor, as is Desi Arnaz, who was a Cuban musician before going into television. Salsa queen Celia Cruz turned her musical career into an acting one thanks to the movie *The Mambo Kings*, in which she starred alongside fellow Latino actor Andy Garcia. Music legend Tito Puente also acted in that film, as did Desi Arnaz Jr., who played the role of his father. Jennifer Lopez is another good example. She started her career as a backup dancer to Janet Jackson before landing the starring role playing Tejano musician Selena Quintanilla in the film *Selena*. From there she crossed over into music where she has again been very successful.

Desi Arnaz

In years past, it was common for Latino performers to adopt Anglo-sounding names in an attempt to hide their heritage and escape the discrimination rampant in the theater and film business. Today, more and more Latino performers are embracing their names and heritage as things to be open about and proud of. Other famous actors and actresses who have Latino roots include: Martin Sheen and his sons Charlie Sheen and Emilio Estevez, Cameron Diaz, Freddie Prinze Jr., Jessica Alba, Jimmy Smits, and Raquel Welch. Another famous Latino actor, Raul Julia, actually got his start with a small Latino theater company before working his way up to major musical productions and movies.

The ties between famous Latinos in the arts extend beyond just music and dance. *The Mambo Kings*, for example, was based on a book by Cuban Oscar Hijuelos. El Teatro Campesino founder Luis Valdez moved into the movie business and directed the 1987 hit *La Bamba*, a movie based on the life of Latino rocker Ritchie Valens. Mexican artist Frida Kahlo has also been portrayed on screen in the movie *Frida*, in which she was played by Latina actress Salma Hayek. *Frida* was written and directed by another Latino, Gregory

Jennifer Lopez

Nava, who was also involved in the production of *El Norte*—a film about Guatemalan immigrants for which he was nominated for an Oscar Award—and *My Family*—a film focusing on Mexican culture and family. These last two movies are excellent examples of a new wave of Latino films that deal with deep cultural issues and portray Latinos in a realistic rather than a stereotypical light. Given the power of film and television to educate and expose audiences to unfamiliar cultures and places, it is important that this trend continue if American society as a whole is to have a full understanding of Latinos rather than a shallow, negative, and stereotypical one.

Carnivals and Festivals

A Day of the Dead altar

y now you have had a chance to learn a little about several different forms of Latino art. Quite often, each of these art forms appears separately: paintings are in museums, plays are in theaters, stories are in books, music is on the radio, and dance is performed in ballrooms or shows. All of these kinds of artistic expression, however, are tied together by the culture they belong to. One of the times they all come together is during cultural festivals, and these offer a very good opportunity to become familiar with Latino art. Let's take a look at some of the most prominent Latino festivals held in the United States and explore how various art forms are used to celebrate and communicate culture.

Día de los Muertos

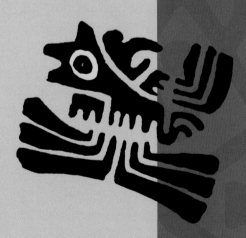

ía de los Muertos, or Day of the Dead, is a Mexican holiday celebrated on November 2. It is a tradition that dates back to before the arrival of Columbus. The roots of the celebration come from the Native peoples, particularly the Aztecs, and have been modified over time to embrace Christian influences. It is believed that, on this day, the souls of the dead return to be with their families. For this special occasion, each family builds an altar to their loved ones and decorates the altar

motif: *a theme in art or literature.*

Much of the artwork associated with Día de los Muertos is created as an *ofrenda*, or "offering," to the deceased. This includes artistically created food, paper flowers made by children, beadwork, carvings, paintings, or just about any other form of art you could mention.

with pictures, flowers, candles, food, and items that were important to the dead person during his life. The altar helps the family remember their relative and helps guide the dead soul back home.

Día de los Muertos is not meant to be a sad or mournful day. It is a day of remembrance in which families visit, decorate, tell stories of those who have passed away, and even picnic at the gravesites. It is also a day to celebrate life, particularly the lives of children. For that reason, gifts are exchanged. Often the gifts are food with a death *motif*, like artfully made sugar cookies shaped like skulls or *pan de los muertos* (bread of the dead). Sculptures, paintings, and costumes are also created in honor of the dead. Among the festival's most well-known images are the *calacas*—adults dressed as skeletons with carved or molded masks who take children by the hand and dance with them in celebration of the old generations mixing with the new.

In America, Day of the Dead celebrations are often accompanied by festivals that span several days, allowing families to come together to celebrate with each other. In some areas, you do not necessarily have to be of Mexican descent to join in the festivities.

Cinco de Mayo

Cinco de Mayo, or the Fifth of May, is perhaps the most well-known Latino celebration within the United States. It is often confused with Mexican Independence Day, but the two are different occasions (Mexico's Independence Day is actually celebrated on September 16). Cinco de Mayo is a holiday celebrated in honor of a battle in 1862. La Batalla de Puebla, as that battle is known, saw 4,500 Mexican soldiers defeat a better-equipped French Army of 6,500 at the city of Puebla, Mexico. The Mexicans fought under General Ignacio Zaragosa, who was born in Texas and might be looked at today as one of the first Chicano heroes. The holiday was imported to the United States in 1967, during the beginnings of the Chicano movement. A group of Chicano students at California State University decided to do something about the lack of Mexican holidays in America and began their own Cinco de Mayo celebrations.

Today, Cinco de Mayo has become an enormous celebration of Mexican culture, combining foods, music, dance, costumes, artwork, and performances. It is very popular anywhere there are significant Mexican populations, especially along the U.S.-Mexico border, and attracts thousands of people who are not of Mexican descent but who want to join in the festivities.

Dancers at a Latino celebration

Calle Ocho

In the 1960s, Cuba was in the middle of a political revolution, leading many Cubans to flee the country. A large number of these Cuban refugees landed in Miami, Florida, where they made their new homes and formed close-knit Cuban communities. One of those communities was around South West 8th Street, an area that soon became known as Little Havana.

As the years went by, these Cuban immigrants sought a way to celebrate their culture and to make their mark in their new homeland. In 1977, two Cuban Americans from that community, Leslie Pantín Jr. and Willy Bermello, decided to organize

Latino festivals are full of song, dance, and color

a festival that would unite Cubans and put their culture on display. This became Calle Ocho (Eight Street), a Hispanic festival that takes up over twenty city blocks and fills the streets with music, dancing, food, and fun. Though it is still mostly Cuban, other Latino cultures also take part in the celebration. Each year the event is broadcast and photographed by major television networks, radio stations, and newspapers from around the world. The festival draws about a million spectators and is among the largest street parties anywhere in the world.

Carnival

n Catholic cultures, Carnival is celebrated on the day or days leading up to Ash Wednesday—the first day of Lent. Lent, which lasts for the forty days before the beginning of Easter, is a solemn season in which Catholics refrain from indulgences and reflect on their faith and lives. Carnival is like a last big fling before more than a month of restraint and self-control.

Because Catholicism is the dominant religion of Latin America, it is no surprise that in many places in the United States where there are large Latino populations there are also large Latino Carnivals. These celebrations are usually marked with songs and dances, outrageous costumes, and lots of partying. Of course, because not all Catholics are Latinos, not all carnivals will have the same degree of Latino culture and art reflected within them. For example, Mardi Gras, which means Fat Tuesday, is a carnival that takes place the Tuesday before Ash Wednesday. The words "Mardi Gras" are actually French, and the celebration is not a Latino one, even though its origins are Catholic.

There are many other Latino festivals in America celebrating all kinds of different occasions. If you are interested in joining in on the fun, there is probably a celebration near you that will give you the chance to experience Latino culture for yourself.

The word "carnival" is a Latin word meaning "goodbye to meat" and comes from the tradition of avoiding eating meat during the Lenten season.

Habla Español

pelicula (pay-lee-coo-lah): film

cine (see-nay): theater

celebración (say-lay-bra-see-own): celebration

A New
"New World"?

In this book we have talked a lot about communities, cultures, and the role art plays in communicating ideas. As we have seen, culture is something that can be hard to describe. Nevertheless, it is a powerful force in molding individual identities and affecting the way one group interacts with another. Latino culture has always had an influence in the United States, and Latino art has been very important in communicating Latino culture to America and to the world.

For a long time, however, Latino communities have lived on the fringes of American society. Their voices have often gone unheard, and the art that tells the Latino story is only beginning to be recognized as part of the larger American story. As we have seen, Latinos have had a big impact in the United States all along, but most of the attention they have received has come in the world of music and dance and from "Latin Explosion" to "Latin Explosion."

Things are now changing in America in a major way. The Latino community's influence is growing. Latinos are now the largest and fastest-growing minority group in America. Latinos are also one of the youngest population groups in America, meaning that they will become more influential as the young generations grow older and make their mark on the world. In fact, about one-third of Latinos in the United States are under the age of eighteen. As these children grow older and have kids of their own, the Latino population will continue to get bigger. As the Latino population grows larger, it moves further from the fringes and closer to the mainstream of American society. Not only will Latinos themselves make a difference, but mainstream media organizations, magazines, newspapers, TV shows, filmmakers, and advertisers will all have to respond to the interests of Latino people in order to be successful. The recent trends we have seen in music and film, with more Latino artists and subject matter, will continue and even accelerate, and the market for Spanish-language products will also expand. Perhaps most importantly, the greater influence of Latinos in the United States will lead to a change in the way Latinos are viewed by non-Latino Americans, and Latino culture will be understood rather than stereotyped.

The Continuing Importance of Latino Art

As we have seen, one of the best ways for culture to be communicated and understood is through art. Latino art will continue to grow in popularity and will bring with it the stories of a very diverse group of people with a unique perspective. One of the

The "ojo de Dios" (eye of God) is a Hispanic artform that has gained popularity across America.

key features of Latino art is that it is very accessible, which means that Latino communities are eager to share themselves with others and to involve non-Latino people in their art and their celebrations. One of the major things that will help Latino art continue to evolve in America and reach wider audiences is the Internet. Thanks to the Internet, artists who live in communities separated by hundreds or thousands of miles can now communicate with each other easily. This will mean that Latinos in Los Angeles will be able to easily share their ideas and work with Latinos in New York. American Latinos will be able to communicate with people in their Latin American homelands. The result is the

Estimates suggest that there will be 50 million Latinos living in America by the year 2030 and maybe even more.

creation of a virtual community, one made up of people who share cultural ideas and not just geographic location. These on-line communities will also allow people who are not Latino to more easily access Latino culture and gain a better understanding of people they might not otherwise come into contact with.

The "New World" has long been a place where different groups have come together to create new cultures and ideas. The cultures of the Americas are unique in that they are not merely the product of a blending of cultures, but still contain distinct groups with fascinating and diverse histories. Many of these groups, like Latinos, have struggled to find where they belong in the New World. In the new New World, however, there is no doubt that Latino culture is coming into its own and will be a strong force in the world of art and beyond. Soon, the term "Latin Explosion" will be a thing of the past, because Latino art and culture will be very much in the mainstream and there to stay.

Habla Español

communidad (coe-moo-nee-dahd): community

mundo (moon-doe): world

Timeline

1492—Christopher Columbus discovers Española.

1500—Portuguese come to Brazil for the first time.

1791—Saint Domingue slaves start a revolt, leading to their 1804 defeat of the French and the establishment of Haiti.

1917—Citizens of Puerto Rico are given U.S. citizenship.

July 1936—Spanish Civil War begins.

1959—Fidel Castro comes to power in Cuba.

1971—Pablo Neruda wins Nobel Prize for Literature.

1981—Picasso's painting *Guernica* is exhibited in Spain for the first time.

1982—Gabriel García Márquez wins Nobel Prize for Literature.

September 13, 2003—First Latin Grammy Awards is held.

1990—Oscar Hijuelas wins the Pulitzer Prize for Literature for *The Mambo Kings Play Songs of Love*.

1990—Octavio Paz wins Nobel Prize for Literature.

2001—Largest single exhibition of Latino art (organized by Cheech Marin) is launched.

Further Reading

Ancona, George. *Pablo Remembers: The Fiesta of the Day of the Dead.* New York: Lothrop, Lee & Shepard Books, 1993.

Cockroft, James D. and Jane Canning. *Latino Visions: Contemporary Chicano, Puerto Rican, and Cuban American Artists.* New York: Scholastic Press, 2000.

Cruz, Barbara C. *Frida Kahlo: Portrait of a Mexican Painter.* Berkeley Heights, N.J.: Enslow Publishers Inc., 1996.

Heyck, Denis Lynn Daly, ed. *Barrios and Borderlands: Cultures of Latinos and Latinas in the United States.* New York: Routledge, 1994.

Krull, Kathleen. *Harvesting Hope: The Story of Cesar Chavez.* San Diego, Calif.: Harcourt, 2003.

Mirriam-Goldberg, Caryn. *Sandra Cisneros: Latina Writer and Activist.* Berkeley Heights, N.J.: Enslow Publishers Inc., 1998.

Mohr, Nicholasa. *Going Home.* New York: Bantam Books, 1986.

Roberts, John S. *The Latin Tinge: The Impact of Latin American Music on the United States.* Oxford: Oxford University Press, 1998.

Riggs, Thomas, ed. *St. James Guide to Hispanic Artists: Profiles of Latino and Latin American Artists.* Chicago: St. James Press, 2002.

Thomas, Piri. *Down These Mean Streets.* New York: Vintage Books, 1991. (Originally printed in 1967.)

For More Information

Central Arizona/Arizona Republic Day of the Dead Page
www.azcentral.com/ent/dead/history

Calle Ocho Festival Homepage
www.carnaval-miami.org/

Free Online Encyclopedia of Artists
www.artcyclopedia.com

CIA World Factbook
www.cia.gov/cia/publications/factbook/

National Parks Service Web site Containing Information about Chicanos and Muralism
www.cr.nps.gov/history/online_books/5views/5views5e.htm

Online Information About Diego Rivera and Frida Kahlo
www.diego-rivera.org

Online Information About Latino Art in California and the Day of the Dead
www.olvera-street.com

Public Broadcasting System Web site with Information on Latinos and Latino Art
www.pbs.org

Puerto Rican Music
www.musicofpuertorico.com

Thomson-Gale Publishers Biographies of Famous Latinos
www.galegroup.com/free_resources/chh/bio/index.htm

Publisher's note:

The Web sites listed on this page were active at the time of publication. The publisher is not responsible for Web sites that have changed their addresses or discontinued operation since the date of publication. The publisher will review the Web sites and update the list upon each reprint.

Index

Biographies

Rory Makosz was born and raised in Calgary, Alberta, and holds a degree in psychology from Queen's University in Kingston, Ontario. He has been a contributor to *Culture Shock*, a multicultural magazine focused on promoting cultural diversity. He has also written about business, medicine, and ethics. Rory is currently studying law at the University of British Columbia in Vancouver.

Dr. José E. Limón is professor of Mexican-American Studies at the University of Texas at Austin where he has taught for twenty-five years. He has authored over forty articles and three books on Latino cultural studies and history. He lectures widely to academic audiences, civic groups, and K–12 educators.

Picture Credits

Benjamin Stewart: pp. 19, 21, 28, 29, 37, 46, 59, 60, 65, 76, 99, 100, 103

Carin Zissis, carinzissis@hotmail.com: pp. 48, 49

Charles A. Hack: pp. 62, 68

Corel: pp. 9, 10, 11, 12, 22, 73, 82, 85, 88

Dianne Hodack: pp. 6, 8, 24, 40, 58, 70, 90, 102

J. Michael Whittaker, Cuban Art Space: p. 25

José Posada: pp. 77, 79

The Justo A. Martí Photographic Collection, Centro de Estudios Puertorriqueños, Hunter College, CUNY, Photographer unknown: pp. 41, 42, 45, 54, 86, 91

Luis Rodriguez, Cuban Art Space, Center for Cuban Studies: p. 15

Montebravo, Cuban Art Space, Center for Cuban Studies: p. 16

Museum of Spanish Colonial Art, Santa Fe, N.M., Photographer Benjamin Stewart: pp. 27

PhotoDisc: p. 75

Photos.com: pp. 71, 92

The Records of the Offices of the Government of Puerto Rico in the U.S., Centro de Estudios Puertorriqueños, Hunter College, CUNY, Photographer unknown: pp. 52, 93

Rudy Castilla, Centro de Estudios Puertorriqueños, Hunter College, CUNY, Photographer unknown: pp. 55

Sarah Elizabeth Garland: p. 97

Trijillo Weavers, Chimayo, New Mexico, Photographer: Ben Stewart: p. 105